P9-AGF-726

VITAL SIGNS

VITAL SIGNS

Decisions That Determine the Quality of Life and Health

MARK BLOCHER

MOODY PRESS
CHICAGO

© 1992 by
MARK BLOCHER

All rights reserved. No part of this book may be reproduced in any form without permission in writing from the publisher, except in the case of brief quotations embodied in critical articles or reviews.

All Scripture quotations, unless indicated, are taken from the *New American Standard Bible,* © 1960, 1962, 1963, 1968, 1971, 1972, 1973, 1975, and 1977 by The Lockman Foundation, and are used by permission.

Scripture quotations marked (KJV) are taken from the King James Version.

The use of selected references from various versions of the Bible in this publication does not necessarily imply publisher endorsement of the versions in their entirety.

ISBN: 0-8024-9186-3

1 3 5 7 9 10 8 6 4 2

Printed in the United States of America

*To my gifted and gracious wife, Julie,
whose love, patience, godliness, and commitment
to her family have made me a better man.*

*And to my children,
Brian, Sarah, Meagan, and Emily.
Being their father is my greatest accomplishment in life.*

CONTENTS

ACKNOWLEDGMENTS

Many thanks to Michele Martin Shoun, my assistant for the past ten years. Her superb intellect and sharp editing skills helped to shape my thoughts and improve my writing.

Many of the views expressed here were developed while sitting in a fishing boat on Lake Bella Vista with my friend Dave Ewald. His incessant questioning provided an excellent sounding board.

I am grateful to Rex Rogers, Sue Ellen Doenier, Janet Schout, John Ludwig, Ray Paget, Randy Hekman, and my wife, Julie, for their many helpful suggesions (and sometimes brutal honesty). Their critiques have greatly improved the final product.

I also must thank the members of the Baptists for Life executive board, who believed in this project and gave me the freedom to produce it. Finally, I acknowlege the contributions of Victor Matthews and Ronald Mayers, two of my professors at Grand Rapids Baptist College, who managed to take me from being a 1960s hippie to being a philosopher/theologian.

INTRODUCTION

M odern medicine. The term conjures up images of sophisticated machines, white-coated "miracle workers,"
and high-tech operating rooms equipped with the latest gad-
getry.

In the last twenty years there has been a biomedical revolution in Western culture. Whereas manufacturing and mass
production were the giants of the Industrial Revolution, biomedical research and medical manipulation have emerged
as the newest frontier.

Optimism runs high. Surgeries considered impossible a
decade ago are now routine. A "can do" mentality spurs the
belief that there is little or nothing our technological prowess
cannot accomplish. A technological imperative seems to exist that holds that if we can do something about a particular
illness, injury, or disease, we must do it, despite cost or other
limiting factors—even ethics.

But the world of modern medicine is also one where
increasingly difficult decisions are made about who lives and
dies. Sophisticated medical technology improves and extends the lives of many while prolonging the death of others.

Medical technology made Karen Ann Quinlan a house-
hold name in the 1970s. Her parents and doctors believed the
young woman was being kept alive solely by a respirator, a
machine that breathes for people. After a prolonged court
battle, they won the right to turn off the machine, expecting

Karen to die as a result. To everyone's surprise, she lived for another seven years. She not only breathed on her own but maintained a relatively normal pulse and exhibited all other bodily functions we associate with humanness, although she was unconscious and diagnosed as being in a persistent vegetative state.

That case sparked a national debate about using technology to sustain human life. Prior to the introduction of the respirator and other mechanical means of life support, the medical community could do little to resuscitate individuals who stopped breathing or suffered heart attacks or strokes. That situation has changed. Today life support can mean restored life. Or it may mean permanent mental or physical disability, even permanent unconsciousness.

Many people today fear overtreatment. They fear a life merely prolonged by medical "heroics": machines, tubes, wires, and bags of fluids. They fear being kept alive without a "quality of life." And they fear becoming a financial and emotional burden to their families. They want death with "dignity." The question is, are those legitimate concerns? What is medicine, and society, willing to do to guarantee that such fears do not become reality? Even more significant, does the notion of a "quality of life" have biblical support?

And life support is not the only debate in modern medicine. The biomedical revolution has led to the development of medically assisted procreative technologies, such as in vitro fertilization, gamete intrafallopian transfer, zygote intrafallopian transfer, low tubal ovum transfer, artificial insemination, and a range of fertility treatments for infertile couples.

The technological imperative is also evident in the continued development of solid organ substitution technologies. Harvesting organs (as it is known in the industry) is so common that the U.S. government has enacted a Required Request law, which requires hospital personnel to ask every family of potential organ donors to donate the organs of their deceased loved ones. And extensive media campaigns have increased public awareness of the need for organ donations.

However, a debate within the medical community is intensifying regarding the selling of organs, because not enough people are voluntarily donating their organs and the need is continually growing. That shortage gives rise to more questions of ethics. Should an individual who has smoked heavily throughout his adult life receive a heart transplant when others who have taken care of their bodies are waiting? Should an alcoholic receive a liver transplant? Should a person receive an organ transplant regardless of her ability to pay the $45,000 to $150,000 that it costs?

Genetic engineering is another area of concern. Through the use of recombinant DNA technology, agriculturists can now produce beef cattle, chickens, and other livestock quickly, thereby increasing profits and reducing costs. The same technology has been used to produce prescription drugs for conditions such as diabetes. Genetic engineers believe that the application of scientific knowledge can alter the genetics of human beings. They hope to eliminate genetic defects altogether through gene therapy. Yet the question remains, What will that tampering mean to future generations?

WHY THIS BOOK?

This book is designed to help Christians think about some areas where modern medicine and biblical morality seem to conflict. Many aspects of modern medicine raise significant moral issues.

- An unmarried woman requests a prescription for contraception—should a Christian physician comply?
- A Christian woman finds that she is carrying an unborn child with a genetic defect—should she abort?
- Parents have a severely handicapped newborn in the neonatal intensive care unit—do they insist that she be treated?
- An elderly resident of a nursing home suffers a heart attack—should staff resuscitate him?

Parents, spouses, and pastors face such decisions every day. This book is designed to assist believers in assessing current trends in medical practice and addressing the ethical questions they raise. Each chapter focuses on one aspect of medicine and addresses particular problems raised in that area. Suggestions are given for supplemental study. Case studies, questions, and other exercises are included to facilitate further thinking.

HOW TO USE THIS BOOK

1. Sunday school classes or discussion groups could read and discuss one chapter each week for a quarter.
2. Discussion questions are provided as suggestions. Your reading may prompt other questions.
3. Pastors could use this material in discussion with colleagues.
4. Reference materials are listed in the bibliography for further study.

Part 1:
Concerning Right and Wrong

1

FIRST
PRINCIPLES

I was picketing a local abortion clinic, and the security guard came out, so we began talking. Conversation soon centered on how we know right and wrong. He asserted that morals were determined by feelings: "I just know what is right and what is wrong."

I asked him if it was all right for me base my morals on how I felt, too. "Of course," he replied.

So I asked him, "If I felt like taking out a revolver and pumping you full of lead—would that be all right?"

Incredulous, he answered, "No. That would be murder."

"But I felt it was right, Jim. And I have the freedom to act on my feelings since you said that they form the basis of right and wrong."

"Well, shooting me would be against the law and it would be wrong," he responded.

"OK," I said, "I'll just get enough people together who feel the way I do and we'll change the law so that it will be all right to shoot you." Jim quickly reminded me that the U.S. Constitution protects him from such a law.

I replied, "That's no problem. I'll find enough people who feel the way I do, and we'll change the Constitution. What true reason can you give for saying it would be wrong to shoot you?" Jim had no answer to my question.

His silence showed the problem of relativism, the belief that there are no absolutes. When there is no final authority or moral absolutes grounded in that authority, we are left with moral anarchy. Then we are morally and ethically impoverished because we have no fixed point of reference by which to make moral judgments. When we factor in human depravity, it is clear what the consequences can and will be.

Relativism is rejected by believers. The notion that something can be morally right for one person and morally wrong for another has no basis in the Bible. Instead, we learn that if a person is not practicing truth, he is practicing error.

Truth does not come in different sizes. It is not a hat that fits one person but not another. Truth is universal. Everyone, regardless of religious background, education, training, or philosophical views, believes in right and wrong. Whether an individual acknowledges it or not, he conducts his life according to a moral code. No society could exist without a commitment to certain basic values. That applies to atheistic societies as well as those framed by belief in God.

THE FINAL AUTHORITY OF SCRIPTURE

The most important issue to be resolved in moral matters is the question of authority. Upon what criteria are right and wrong—good and evil—decided? How do we know what is right or wrong?

The Bible provides us with an inerrant and infallible source of authority. It is an unchanging court of appeals from which we can always determine right, and it provides us with a sure word of authority on moral issues. Biblical patterns apply to the unbeliever as well as the believer, because there is only one God.

Some argue that that claim constitutes "ramming religion down people's throats." They state that it imposes our own morality on others. Frankly, my morality would not be significantly different from the worst of mankind's because we are all fallen creatures. Our goal must be to seek to impose God's morality. I have no authority to impose my morality on others, but the God of the universe does.

Standards for right and wrong involve more than a Christian's saying, "I believe the Bible." We must know what specific teachings in Scripture shape our morality. Are those principles applicable in every situation, to every generation? What about issues that the Bible does not directly address, such as organ transplants? How do we know what is right in areas where Scripture appears to be silent?

The implications of certain moral precepts, such as the Ten Commandments, are undisputed. They require little interpretation. "Thou shalt not steal" is clear. "Thou shalt not commit adultery" needs no explanation. In addition to the Decalogue are numerous passages in Scripture that express explicit statements concerning individual conduct.

How do we know what to do when the Bible isn't explicit? Believers err in assuming that the Bible is an encyclopedia of moral precepts for all occasions. Although Scripture does teach one how to act in every situation, it does so through general moral principles, not a checklist of dos and don'ts. Scripture does not address every moral problem or situation explicitly.

For instance, the Bible does not directly address the use of mind-altering substances such as heroin or cocaine. But by applying the principle of glorifying God in our bodies (1 Corinthians 6:20), or being controlled by the Spirit rather than by an intoxicating substance (Ephesians 5:18), it is clear that there are some practices in which the believer should not engage.

What about the medical use of narcotics to control pain? Would injecting a wounded soldier with morphine violate biblical admonitions? Many wrongly assume that if the Bible does not address an issue, they are free to decide for themselves. If that assumption were true, the spiritual vitality of the average believer would be destroyed; the fact that the Bible does not address a specific situation does not mean that it says nothing concerning it at all.

Second Timothy 3:16-17 teaches that the Scriptures have been given by God to insure that the man of God is "thoroughly furnished unto all good works" (KJV). God has given us all that is necessary to be fully equipped for a life that pleases Him.

FIRST PRINCIPLES

The Word of God contains clear teachings that enable us to make moral decisions in situations where explicit instructions are absent. I call those teachings First Principles, the foundational teachings of Scripture that help us determine morality.

For example, the Bible does not explicitly denounce the practice of abortion. Some groups, such as the Religious Coalition for Abortion Rights, conclude that that silence means the Bible does not condemn abortion. However, by applying the biblical teaching on the sanctity of human life and the value of children, it is impossible to conclude that the Bible is neutral on abortion.

The following are First Principles we can use to make moral decisions in areas where the Bible is silent.

The Existence of a Sovereign, Self-Revealed, Holy God

Genesis 1:1 states, "In the beginning, God created the heavens and the earth." No comment is made concerning the origin of God. It simply states that He exists. We know Him because He has revealed Himself to us. Romans 1 teaches that God's existence and moral character can be known through nature, or "natural revelation."

Paul also declared that God has placed in every man's conscience an internal law that indicates right and wrong, leaving no one an excuse before Him (Romans 1:20). Where moral precepts that man can know apart from the Bible exist, we are free to legislate those precepts (Romans 2:14-15). We can even "impose morality" in such cases.

Divine Creation of the Universe

God created the heavens and the earth. Scripture asserts that fact numerous times. Genesis 1 and 2 make clear that creation was more than the beginning of an evolutionary process. God spoke the universe into existence with design and purpose.

Believers need to understand that the universe is uniform, specifically designed with order and purpose. Nothing is here by chance. That uniformity of nature reflects God's character (Romans 1:18-20).

Nevertheless, the uniformity of nature exists in an open system. That is, whereas nature operates according to certain laws—gravity, motion, causation—God can intervene to supersede those natural laws. Jesus demonstrated that ability by restoring Lazarus to life, healing the blind and lame, and calming storms. So we must avoid a mechanistic view of the universe that excludes the possibility of divine intervention.

Man as Divine Image Bearer

Rather than being a little higher than the apes, as evolutionists claim, man is a little lower than the angels (Psalm 8:5; Hebrews 2:6-7). Man is not just another part of nature; he is above nature. He is God's vice-regent, exercising stewardship over the earth on God's behalf (Genesis 1:28).

Man's uniqueness is not seen only in his functions (thought, emotion, and will) but in the fact that he is the only created being for whom Christ gave His life. The sacrifice of Christ is the greatest statement regarding the sanctity of human life that could ever be made.

Man bears the stamp of God's image, not because he has certain mental abilities or particular physical capacities but simply by virtue of the fact that he exists. God made man in His own image and likeness. We do not gain image, and we cannot lose it. It cannot be quantified.

That is important to understand in light of the ongoing debate over when a fetus becomes a person or when the soul enters the body. Plato is responsible for the notion that the body is only an instrument of the soul and does not constitute a necessary aspect of "personhood." In fact, Plato taught that the body was the tomb of the soul, a teaching that contributed to the development of "Christian" Gnosticism.

In contrast, Christians believe that man is a unified being, having both a physical and spiritual dimension. The body and spirit are equally important, given the fact that the Lord Jesus died to redeem the total person, not just the spirit. The body will be resurrected and glorified one day. If the body were not important, there would be no need for Christ's bodily resurrection. There would have been no reason for Moses and Elijah's physical appearance on the Mount of Transfiguration. And it would make little sense for us to anticipate the physical return of Christ.

Thus Christians must avoid the practice of referring to unconscious, brain-damaged persons as "vegetables," as if the individual no longer resided in the body. A biblical understanding of personhood means it is not possible to have a living body on earth and a spirit in heaven.

Perhaps a clearer way to describe personhood is to concentrate on relations rather than functions. We are image bearers by virtue of our relationship to God. We are persons because we are His image, not because we can think, feel, and exercise our will. Being human places one in relationship to God.

For example, when a woman gives birth to a child, that child does not have to earn the right to be her child; he is already her child. Even though the newborn has not fully developed or manifested a personality, the child is distinctly hers by virtue of their relationship, biologically and socially.

In the same sense, God relates to us from an eternal perspective. He knew us before the foundations of the world (1 Peter 1:20). He declares us "image" (Genesis 1:26) because that is what we are, not what we become. Imaging God is the essence of being human. However, our depravity seeks to eliminate that reality. Not content to be the image of God, we seek to be God Himself.

It is not appropriate to suppose that there are two separate categories of human beings: potential image bearers and actual image bearers. It is appropriate to acknowledge that we are all actual image bearers who are on our way to realizing our potential.

Thus the microscopic, preimplantation human embryo is as much an eternal "person" as a sixty-five-year-old. Personhood does not depend on size, age, or location; it is synonymous with "image bearer" and "human being." One cannot be a human being without being a person or image bearer.

The Reality of the Fall

The clear teaching of Scripture is that man and the universe are in a fallen condition as a result of man's rebellion in the Garden of Eden (Genesis 3). For his sin, man was sentenced to death. That sentence is also applied to the rest of creation. Man is not perfectible in his fallen state; he is not even improving, as some would like to believe. And in the normal course of events, people die, regardless of advances in modern medicine. "It is appointed for men to die once, and after this comes judgment" (Hebrews 9:27).

However, man's depraved condition does not render him incapable of doing good to or for others. Nor does it mean that every person is as sinful as he or she could be or that everyone engages in every possible form of sin. It does mean that we are incapable of earning favor with God. Our relationship with Him as divine image bearers has been fractured. Our part in the relationship is characterized by alienation rather than communion. Consequently, we "suppress the truth in unrighteousness" (Romans 1:18), refusing to acknowledge God as our Creator. We worship the creation rather than the Creator (Romans 1:21-23).

Total depravity means that our bodies are in a state of deterioration. In the language of the Second Law of Thermodynamics, matter moves from a higher state to a lower state. Such deterioration, apart from the supernatural working of God, is irreversible. Our physical frames are in a perpetual state of disintegration. Despite the best and most sincere efforts of medical research, man in his fallen state is not immortal. Physicians may extend life by replacing organs and other means, but in the end death is inevitable. Disease, disability, and illness are integral to the human experience.

We should never forget man's intrinsically sinful nature. It is our nature to function contrary to the laws of God. Although that nature may not be fully manifested in every situation, it must always be considered. Humanitarian goals and motives should not charm us into acceptance of therapies and treatments that undermine biblical teachings. It is not enough to say that a particular invention will save lives or that a particular research project will benefit many people. A noble end does not justify means. The Dachau hypothermia experiments conducted by the Nazis on Jewish prisoners may have provided significant data for saving lives, but we can hardly ignore the source of that research, nor can we erase the immorality of abusing unwilling subjects. The Nuremburg Code of Medical Ethics is quite clear on this matter.

The Universal Application of the Biblical Pattern of Human Sexuality, Marriage, and Family

God made male and female in His image. Adam and Eve, our first parents, were created sexual beings; therefore, sexuality is a normal and necessary part of human existence.

Scripture teaches that the only appropriate expression of sexuality is between one man and one woman who are married to each other for life. Homosexuality, bestiality, adultery, and premarital sexual involvement unarguably fall outside the biblical pattern (Exodus 20:14; 22:19; Romans 1:26-27; 1 Corinthians 6:18). Scripture is clear that sexuality is God's gift for married couples as both a means of procreation and an expression of intimacy and oneness in the relationship.

That principle applies to Christians and non-Christians alike, which is an important point when we consider the various expressions of human sexuality in Western culture. God does not have two different sets of standards—one for His children and one for everyone else. His standards are not based on us humans but on His own holy character.

Marriage was designed by God to be a lifelong commitment of one man to one woman. "For this cause a man shall leave his father and his mother, and shall cleave to his wife; and they shall become one flesh" (Genesis 2:24). Divorce is a deviation from that pattern, as is cohabitation without marriage. History can attest to the obvious, natural consequences for violating that pattern. Consider how much harm has come to individuals who did not follow it—how many children have been torn between two warring parents, how much pain has been caused by marital infidelity. The natural consequences of deviating from the biblical pattern are also seen in the epidemic numbers of unwed mothers, abortions, sexually transmitted diseases, and deaths from AIDS.

CONCLUSION

The way we use our God-given abilities in the field of medicine is crucial; the stakes are high. We cannot afford to be driven by technology. Rather, we must practice principles taught in Scripture. Modern culture may well continue to slide into moral oblivion and chaos because of man's refusal to acknowledge laws higher than his own and the fact that moral precepts spring from a personal God. However, Christians, whether engaged in health care professions or not, should not accept the moral schizophrenia that increasingly characterizes modern medical practice. We should not be afraid to say "Thus saith the Lord" in upholding God's standards of morality.

QUESTIONS TO THINK ABOUT

1. How do we make moral decisions?
2. How can we determine the rightness of an action that is not explicitly addressed in Scripture?
3. Can a decision be moral for one person and immoral for another?
4. Is there room for "Christian liberty" in cases where the Bible is not explicit about an issue?

2

TRADITIONAL PRINCIPLES OF MEDICAL ETHICS

In Utopia men and women would be guided by an innate sense of right and wrong, perfectly harmonizing together and guided by an established, unchanging moral consensus. There would be no need for laws or rules or kings.

However, in a fallen world, individuals' desires, dreams, and motives produce conflict not only with other people but also within themselves. Laws, rules, and guiding principles are necessary to make society civil. Without them, fallen humanity would readily exhibit its inhumanity, and society would dissolve into a state of moral anarchy.

In the previous chapter we studied some guiding principles as established by God, the Creator of all men and women. Those laws are followed imperfectly by imperfect men, resulting in something less than perfection. Yet they provide an unfailing, consistent scheme for living. In this chapter we will examine man's best rules for governing medicine. It must be pointed out at the start that these are the flawed product of flawed men. Although high-minded, inherently they lead to conflict. Any one of the four principles spelled out here, when taken to the extreme, will find itself in opposition to the other three.

Even the most ardent advocate of evolution, who believes human existence is the result of chance, will agree that certain moral principles guide the actions of men. As discussed in the previous chapter, all men are guided by some concept of right and wrong, although what is considered wrong in one situation may be considered right in another. Although there is no universal consensus on what those guiding principles are, the agreement is that some actions can be labeled good or bad.

All concepts of morality involve the idea that man is autonomous, capable of making moral decisions. The notion of morality presupposes that the rightness or wrongness of particular actions can be known and taught. Were that not the case, it would be difficult to enact laws or establish any standards of conduct. How would anyone govern if there were not at least minimal consensus about right and wrong? How could we legislate theft of property or bodily injury if there did not exist some basic moral consensus?

The practice of human medicine has operated upon a particular set of moral principles for centuries, principles that govern decision making and medical practice. These principles are: autonomy, nonmaleficence, beneficence, and justice.

AUTONOMY

The principle of autonomy projects man as a competent decision maker, capable of determining what is or is not in his own best interest. The term autonomy joins two Greek words, *autos*, meaning self, and *nomos*, meaning rule. Autonomy literally means "self-rule." It has become synonymous with the right of individuals to choose for themselves, to enjoy personal privacy, and to assume personal responsibility.

American culture reveres the notion of individual autonomy, as evidenced by our Bill of Rights. Personal freedom is also enshrined in the U.S. Constitution.

In medicine, respect for a patient's autonomy drives our belief that an individual should be asked for his or her consent before medical treatment is provided. People have the right to be informed of their physical condition, what treatments are available, and the risks of proposed treatments. Once informed, the individual has the right to grant or refuse consent for a particular treatment, since he knows his own self-interest best.

Informed consent assumes that a person has the capacity to understand the information he receives and the ability to give voluntary consent. From a legal standpoint, it means that he has reached legal adulthood, and the law considers him to be a competent decision maker. When a patient is not a legal adult, consent must be provided by a parent or guardian.

Competence is also an issue in informed consent since many legal adults lack the mental or physical ability to participate in decision making. An unconscious or mentally impaired person is unable to comprehend the facts or make an informed decision. Thus, another person will exercise "substituted judgment" on his or her behalf.

The opposite of autonomy, paternalism, assumes a patient is either incapable of making a decision or is unable to understand the information. If a doctor proceeds with an operation without obtaining informed consent, perhaps because he feels the patient would not comprehend the information, his behavior is considered paternalistic. Informed consent is more than a signature on a consent form; it involves true understanding. Even when a signature has been obtained, if the patient does not understand the true nature of the procedure and the reasons for it, the physician is practicing paternalism.

In recent years, autonomy has justified practices that were once abhorred by both society in general and the medical community in particular. Abortion, once considered murder by physicians, is now regarded as a woman's constitutional right. Physicians in 1972 who performed abortions faced criminal prosecution. Today an abortion is considered a procedure like any other basic health service. To inform a female patient where an abortion could be obtained used to be viewed as being an accessory to murder in some states. Today physicians who are prevented from informing their patients about abortion claim that is a violation of their right to free speech; such prevention is considered an intrusion into the doctor-patient relationship.

Likewise, autonomy arguments are used to defend assisted suicide for terminally ill patients. In the past, a person expressing a death wish, or attempting to take his own life, would have been considered mentally incompetent and placed on a suicide watch. It was thought that anyone who wanted to die was out of touch with reality. But now with the advocacy of Jack Kervorkian ("Dr. Death") and the advent of suicide manuals such as *Final Exit*, by Derek Humphrey, the founder of the Hemlock Society, suicide is no longer considered incompatible with mental competence. A person can now refuse medical life-saving treatment or request help from a physician to end his life "humanely."

NONMALEFICENCE

The principle of nonmaleficence precludes physicians from harming their patients, better known as "first do no harm" (*primum non nocere*). The Hippocratic Oath recognized that a physician's foremost duty was to avoid harming his patient.

Nonmaleficence figures prominently in medical malpractice lawsuits, since modern tort law involves such matters as negligence, personal injury, and compensation. When a physician injures a patient through negligence or malice, he has breached his obligation to avoid harm. The failure to conduct a medical exam that would have revealed a threat to a patient's health is as much a breach of this ethic as performing unnecessary surgery.

When a patient with AIDS asks his or her physician not to reveal the diagnosis to others, does the physician harm the patient by telling the family? Or is the family harmed by not being told? Which constitutes harm?

Tragically, physicians are sued today if they are unwilling to conduct exams that might reveal a defective unborn child. Public morality has changed to such a degree that courts award large monetary judgments to people whose children are born with handicaps. The result is that those physicians who are unwilling to conduct "search and destroy missions" on unborn patients are punished.

The difference between "killing" and "letting die" is another area where the principle of nonmaleficence applies. When a patient is in extreme pain, does the physician have a duty to kill her, especially when she is unable to ask him to do so? In the Netherlands, many physicians believe they have a duty to kill their dying patients. Petr Admirraal, leading advocate of the Dutch euthanasia movement, believes dying patients have a right to be killed. He believes physicians should consider it their obligation to put terminally ill patients "out of their misery." Is the principle of nonmaleficence violated by a physician's withholding or withdrawing a treatment with the intent to hasten death?

BENEFICENCE

Beneficence implies that a physician has a duty to take actions that contribute to the welfare of his patients. He is obligated to provide assistance that eliminates or reduces harm. The Hippocratic tradition requires physicians to utilize their skills for the benefit of their patients.

Obviously, that implies positive acts on the part of physicians. In essence, the obligation is to provide only those treatments and therapies that contribute to the patient's well-being. Excessive or unnecessary treatment that serves no purpose other than padding the physician's income is a flagrant violation of this principle.

In recent times, the principle has undergone dramatic change. Aborting a child because it was unplanned or untimely is now considered rendering a benefit. But who does it benefit? Certainly not the unborn child. Removing organs from "brain dead" accident victims is now viewed as honoring this principle of beneficence. Even starving a person who is permanently unconscious is sometimes considered rendering a benefit, assuming that death is preferable to unconscious existence.

Therefore, nonmedical issues are increasingly factored into medical decisions. Economics and quality of life are often given equal or greater weight as the issue of direct physical benefit to the patient. For example, deciding whether to place an elderly heart attack victim on a respirator is sometimes based on the patient's finances, health insurance coverage, expected quality of life, and his family's wishes. The fact that the respirator would provide a direct medical benefit sometimes gets lost in the shuffle.

It is true that beneficence cannot be completely blind to all other factors since medical resources are not infinite. An intensive care unit may have a limited number of respirators (at least theoretically—most ICUs can contact a medical supply company and rent more if necessary), and decisions may have to be made regarding who gets the last one. However, that would be more an issue of distributive justice than of beneficence. If nine patients need a respirator and each would benefit from it, in the event of a shortage the issue is allocation, not beneficence.

Risk is also a factor in assessing benefit. Seldom does a therapy offer a benefit that is entirely risk free. For example, administering narcotics to control postoperative pain provides temporary relief, but with each additional dosage the potential for physical dependence increases. Sometimes the benefit is only temporary, and the risks increase each time the benefit is provided.

JUSTICE

In *The Babylonian Lottery*, Jorge Luis Borges describes a society in which all social burdens and benefits are distributed by lottery. Each time the lottery is conducted, a person might end up a slave, factory owner, priest, executioner, or prisoner. One could be fabulously wealthy and then as poor as dirt. Past contributions to society, humanitarian achievements, and so on are completely irrelevant. All benefits and burdens are distributed impartially by the random selection of the lottery.

Most of us would find such a process repulsive, largely because we believe in the just distribution of benefits and burdens. However, ask any group of people what would constitute just distribution, and you will receive a wide variety of answers. How do we determine justice?

Our concept of justice arises from a notion of fairness. Fairness is important in our culture, given the urgency with which most people assert individual rights. Most believe no one should shoulder more than his or her share of burdens. In an ideal world, everyone shoulders an equal weight.

However, we do not live in an ideal world. So whose sense of justice should we use? When there are competing claims for the last bed in an intensive care unit or for the remaining kidney dialysis machine, who decides which patient receives care and which one does not? Should the person with the ability to pay preempt the one with limited financial resources? Should social standing be a valid criterion?

CONCLUSIONS

The traditional principles that guide medical practice are in themselves insufficient to provide a consistent health care ethic. That is because man is not basically good, man's physical frame is not perfectible, and we do not operate in a closed system. Man is not the measure of all things.

Additionally, those principles are useless apart from a consensus within society to apply them and to punish violators. Past generations of physicians enjoyed such a consensus, which was predicated on a Judeo-Christian worldview. They shared a belief that man is more than a body, that there is life after death, and that men are accountable for their actions. But that consensus no longer exists.

Until now, courses in medical ethics were unnecessary in medical school because there was an awareness that physicians should respect patients and seek their benefit. That has changed. Today patients cannot assume that their physician will be an uncompromising advocate for their welfare. Similarly, physicians cannot assume patients will be unreservedly grateful. The conflicts emerging from this social change constitute the remainder of this book.

Part 2:
Issues in Human Procreation

3

CONCEPTION CONTROL AND FAMILY SIZE

How many children should the average American couple have? The answer remains elusive in a culture of conflicting values and priorities. Some argue that current population and environmental concerns call for smaller families. Others contend that we should not even raise the question but simply be open to whatever children we may procreate. One thing is certain—within the Christian community there is little agreement about the use of conception control and family size.

Conception control (methods that prevent conception as contrasted with birth control, which prevents a birth) is a common practice among Christians. More use it than don't. However, if my conversations with Christians throughout the U.S. are any indication, few have really thought through why they use conception control or how it actually works.

This chapter is written to provide a framework for considering the issues surrounding conception control and family size. It is not my intention to speak "ex cathedra" and declare the biblical position. I am not the Holy Spirit, and it is not my desire, nor is it my role, to make people feel guilty for their practices or motives. However, I do believe there are some profound implications for the family, the church, and society if Christian couples continue to practice conception control in the same manner and for the same reasons as the general population.

WHOSE CHILDREN ARE THEY ANYWAY?

The key question is not how many children should we have, but where do children come from? Who gives us children to rear and why? Biblically, we understand that children are born of the one-flesh relationship between husband and wife (Genesis 2:24). God gives us children. Human beings do not merely breed; they procreate, cooperating with God in the perpetuation of others who are made in God's image. No parent owns her children. They are not property but lives loaned by God. As one person has said, "Children are the messages we send to a generation we will never see."

God never gives children to punish people. When we see a pregnant woman we ought not despair, as if pregnancy were the end of happiness. The tragedy of out-of-wedlock pregnancy is not the pregnancy—it is that two people robbed themselves of God's best for their lives. Pregnancy is not sin; illicit sexual involvement is. However, even in such a circumstance God does not allow a child to be conceived in order to punish the sinning parents. In fact, He will use the situation to bring glory to Himself.

If I communicate any message at all it is that children are a blessing, that motherhood and fatherhood are blessings, that God entrusts parents with children to rear in such a manner that those children will worship Him and teach their children to do the same. I am not as concerned about the actual use of conception control as I am about the attitudes conception control has fostered toward children.

Modern Western culture is awash with examples of children being alienated from their parents. Teen suicide, drug abuse, and illicit sexual relations are symptoms of kids being alienated from adults. It seems that the more control humans have gained over procreation, the more neglected and alienated from parents the children have become. Having the power to prevent conception seems to have fostered the idea that children exist to satisfy the needs and desires of adults.

Jesus said, "And whosoever shall offend one of these little ones that believe in me, it is better for him that a millstone were hung about his neck, and he were cast into the sea" (Mark 9:42, KJV). That verse makes clear how the Lord Jesus Christ views children. Shouldn't we have a similar attitude?

THE HISTORY OF BIRTH CONTROL

From where does the notion of limiting the size of our families come? Birth control is not a new phenomenon. Interest in controlling conception can be traced back thousands of years. Archaeologists and historians have found evidence that the ancient Egyptians practiced various forms of conception control. Greeks and Romans engaged in a variety of practices aimed at preventing conception as well. Voluntary childlessness was common in the Roman Empire as were the practices of abortion and infanticide. More recent Western history finds abortion and primitive forms of conception control in use in the U.S. as early as the 1800s.

Throughout church history, however, Christians have taken a stand against the elimination and limitation of children. Early theologians such as Augustine, Tertullian, and Irenaeus wrote against such practices. Nations influenced by Christianity saw increases in their population and in the "quality of life" their citizens enjoyed. Our own culture is an example of what a nation with a high regard for children and family can produce. For the most part, American history reflects the role that Judeo-Christian values concerning marriage, family, and morality have played in making America the wealthiest and most generous nation in the history of mankind. History will also show what happened when the nation turned its back on God's principles.

It was not until 1930 that any U.S. church body accepted artificial means of conception control, and that was an extremely cautious position. That year, the bishops of the American Anglican Church at the Lambeth Conference stated,

> Where there is a clearly felt moral obligation to limit or avoid parenthood, the method must be decided on Christian principles. . . . Where there is a morally sound reason for avoiding complete abstinence, the conference agrees that other

> methods may be used, provided that this is done in light of
> the same Christian principles. The Conference records its
> strong condemnation of the use of any conception control
> through motives of selfishness, luxury, or mere convenience.[1]

That statement reflects the bishops' concern that artificial
conception control could violate biblical principles and be
abused by Christians. The caution against using conception
control for "luxury or mere convenience" seems prophetic in
light of present practice.

Other church bodies soon followed that cautious endorsement. Today only the Roman Catholic Church main-
tains a position against artificial conception control. Since
1930 the Protestant community, particularly the Reformed tradition, has engaged in a fairly vigorous debate on the issue,
especially during the 1960s as "the Pill" gained popularity.
However, Christians from virtually every denominational tradition engage in contraceptive practice. It is clearly the rule
rather than the exception.

Public and Christian attitudes toward childbearing and
motherhood have changed significantly since the 1960s,
when it was still common to hear a birth described as a
"blessed event." In today's culture, many consider pregnancy
almost a disease. Willard Cates, director of the abortion sur-
veillance project for the National Centers for Disease Control
in Atlanta, Georgia, called pregnancy "a moderately extended, chronic condition, an illness to be treated by evacuation
of the uterine contents. From a strict medical perspective, all
pregnancies should be terminated."[2] Warren Hern, a physician who specializes in late-term abortions in Boulder, Colorado, refers to pregnancy as a "disease." The rhetoric of
abortion rights advocates frequently means depicting pregnancy as an abnormal state.

The use of contraception has become so commonplace
even among Christians that arguments against it are literally
viewed as alien. In the twenty years that I have been a Christian I have never heard a sermon on the numbering and spacing of children or the use of artificial means of conception
control. In premarital counseling sessions, couples are likely

to be asked what kind of conception control they will use, not whether they plan to use it.

Pastors, sometimes even those in their twenties or early thirties, obtain vasectomies, and their wives tubal ligations. The same is no doubt true of people in the pews.

When did attitudes about sex and childbearing change? When did the notion of limiting the size of one's family come to be considered an important part of Christian stewardship? Where did people get the idea that they should separate sexuality from procreation?

A BIBLICAL VIEW OF
HUMAN SEXUALITY AND MARRIAGE

It is no secret that the modern view of sexuality is primarily nonprocreative, that is, sexual relations are primarily for personal fulfillment and gratification. Sex is used to sell products and to attract television viewers and magazine readers. It is viewed as a source of entertainment and humor. Sex-ploitation, masquerading as freedom, is commonplace in America, as the Clarence Thomas/Anita Hill controversy illustrated. Pornography flourishes largely because many have adopted a view of sexuality that focuses on gratification rather than edification. "Recreational sex," a term coined by the experimental generation of baby boomers, manifested itself in the so-called "swinger" lifestyles of the 1970s, with "open marriages," wife swapping, and free-love communes. Today, although the public calls for "safe sex" (what some Christians call "careful promiscuity"), the notion that sexuality is more than a physical experience seems lost on many people. AIDS and other sexually transmitted diseases have created concern among the "sexually active," but the public's appetite for sex continues unabated. However, this free-for-all approach to sex has not produced a happier, healthier people with relationships of increased longevity. Instead, the opposite has occurred, which is what always happens when God's design is perverted.

Biblically, human sexuality is presented as God's gift to married couples, which they may legitimately open on their wedding night. God made us male and female, which means He made us sexual beings. Sexual feelings are a normal part of human existence. However, the only relationship in which the Bible endorses the expression of these sexual feelings is within the confines of a lifelong marriage commitment between a man and woman.

Sex in marriage is one of the key means God has ordained for the development of intimacy between husband and wife (Genesis 2:24). The need for intimacy within marriage is so basic that the only other relationship to compare it with is the relationship between Christ and the church (Ephesians 5:25-33). However, sexual relations are not the only means by which marital intimacy can be achieved. In some instances health or other factors prevent a couple from engaging in sexual relations. Does that mean they are unable to experience intimacy? Probably not.

Sexual relations are one means of developing intimacy. However, Scripture is quite clear on the fact that to attempt to develop that intimacy illegitimately is to defraud someone—it is offering something that you cannot legitimately give away. For example, if I offer to give my neighbor your new Oldsmobile, I am defrauding him because your car is not something I can legitimately give away. Likewise, to offer sexual favors to someone other than my wife is to defraud that other person as well as my wife. My expression of my sexuality is to be reserved only for my wife.

Even within marriage it is possible to defraud one's mate through sexual relations. We are never to be totally ruled by our passions and appetites, whether they be for food or for sex. We are to act only in ways that honor God. Whatever we do, even in such mundane tasks as eating and drinking, we are to bring glory to God (1 Corinthians 10:31). Shouldn't we also seek to glorify God in an area as important as sexuality?

First Thessalonians 4:3-6 teaches that Christians are not to engage in fornication. Each one should learn how to control his passion in a way that will bring honor to God. In verse 4, Paul states that "every one of you should know how to possess his vessel in sanctification and honour" (KJV). Some believe *vessel* refers to the individual's body and that Paul is exhorting the Thessalonian believers to exercise self-control. In fact, that interpretation is incorporated into the NIV translation. However, the context and grammar suggest that vessel is used in reference to the spouse (cf. 1 Peter 3:7). In both Peter's and Paul's writings there is the implication that it is possible to defraud one's marriage partner. Treating one's mate as merely a means to satisfy passion could arguably be viewed as defrauding, just as using someone else to meet sexual needs would be. God places marital sexual relations on a high plane, unlike modern culture's "If it feels good, do it" mentality. According to the Scripture, sexuality is not simply another bodily appetite. Even when sex is experienced within the confines of a monogamous, heterosexual marriage relationship, that does not free us to use our partner's body in any way we wish. A husband does considerable damage to the intimacy his wife seeks when he treats her like a piece of flesh for his own selfish satisfaction. Although the relationship may meet biblical standards, the means of relating may not.

The development of intimacy is not the only reason God created men and women with sexual needs. Sexuality is also important for the propagation of the human race. However, man is distinguished from animals in that humans do not merely breed in order to perpetuate the species. We procreate, that is, we engage in a divine-human cooperative that results in bringing eternal image bearers into existence. Let me stress that procreation is one aspect of marital sexual relations, not the only purpose.

If sex within marriage were to be reserved exclusively for procreation, then infertile couples and those who are postmenopausal would be required to abstain from sexual relations. However, Paul stated that husbands and wives are to not refrain from sexual relations except for a specific period of time and for specific reasons—prayer and fasting (1 Corinthians 7:5). It should be obvious that Paul understood the ramifications of couples' faithfully following these principles. Regular, "unprotected" sex would result in conception and childbirth on some occasions.

Our discussion of human sexuality is important for our consideration of conception control because those who promote Western-style family planning programs have a distorted view of human sexuality and its intended purpose. The prominent advocates of conception control throughout this century have not been theologians or Christian ethicists. If anything, they have been hostile to Christian values. Consequently, Christians cannot blindly accept their views and proposals as advancing biblical ends.

CONTRACEPTIVE METHODS AND CHRISTIAN ETHICS

Any exploration of specific methods of contraception will render much of the controversy around it moot. That is because some methods violate the principle of the sanctity of human life because they prevent not conception but the full development of a human being.

Is there abortion in your medicine chest? Some contraceptives are actually contragestative, that is, they begin working after gestation (pregnancy) has begun. Thus, what you may think prevents conception in reality prevents a fertilized egg from being implanted in the wall of the uterus or developing fully. Drugs and devices that destroy the fertilized egg or prevent implantation are not contraceptives—they are abortifacients. They either kill directly or cause the death of unborn human beings by disrupting the environment necessary for full gestation.

Intrauterine Devices (IUDs)

In the early 1970s large numbers of women, including Christians, allowed physicians to implant intrauterine devices (IUD) to control fertility. Unfortunately the average woman knew little about how they worked. Subsequent research has demonstrated that whereas the IUD may interfere with sperm transport or prevent the egg from entering the uterus, the primary means of operation is the disruption of embryo implantation, which means that the IUD is not a contraceptive but an abortifacient—it kills a developing human being. In light of that fact, a Christian should not use an IUD.

However, many Christian women used IUDs in the past without knowing their true means of operation. Some have expressed feelings of guilt because they allowed a device to be placed in their body that could have ended a human life. Like postabortive women, those women's feelings must be taken seriously. Scripture shows that God is moved by the contrite heart (Psalm 51:17), and He will forgive and cleanse us when we confess our sin.

The Pill

Oral contraceptives are the most widely used form of birth control, with the possible exception of condoms. This form of birth control has been in use for nearly three decades and continues to be the subject of further research.

A growing number of medical authorities, including those who favor abortion, admit that the Pill may act as an abortifacient as well as a contraceptive. The Pill's scope of action may not be limited to preventing conception but may, like the IUD, prevent the implantation of a fertilized egg on the wall of the uterus when break-through ovulation occurs.[3] Sometimes high doses of oral contraceptives are purposely given to women to cause early abortions. They are known as "morning-after pills."

Women who take oral contraceptives are often led to think they prevent conception 100 percent of the time by preventing ovulation, when in reality they may be preventing a newly conceived human being from implanting on the uterine wall. Perhaps ninety-nine out of one hundred times the drug prevents conception, but what of the one time it doesn't?

Admittedly, the research is not conclusive that oral contraceptives such as the so-called mini-pill or low estrogen pill ever function as abortifacients; but neither is research conclusive that they don't. The occurrence of break-through ovulation is fairly conclusively proved. So it doesn't take a scientist to know that when such ovulation occurs and the woman engages in sexual intercourse, conception is a possibility. Studies indicate that the lining of the uterus is altered by the use of oral contraceptives, which means that when break-through ovulation and conception occur, the uterine wall may be inhospitable to the embryo.

My problem with oral contraception is that since the possibility of disrupting implantation does exist, even if the chances are 1 in 1,000, a woman cannot use the Pill with confidence that it is 100 percent contraceptive. Some may respond that that is not a sufficiently compelling reason not to use oral contraceptives since there are other things people use that can cause death but we still use them, such as automobiles. People are killed by cars, but does that mean we shouldn't drive a car because it might cause someone's death? Cars do kill people, but that is not the reason they exist. Oral contraceptives, however, exist solely to prevent a person from coming into existence. They are intended to prevent life from beginning. If they also have the secondary function of preventing an embryo from developing, then their effectiveness is enhanced, not diminished. Automakers are not pleased when their cars kill people. However, to my knowledge, the manufacturers of oral contraceptives are not bothered by the prospect of their product preventing implantation of a living embryo.

Whereas the scientific research may not be conclusive that the Pill occasionally acts as an abortifacient, advocates of abortion claim that it does. In oral arguments before the U.S. Supreme Court in *Webster v. Reproductive Health Services*, Frank Susman, the attorney representing the abortion providers in Missouri, argued that if the Court upheld the Missouri statute that placed restrictions on abortion, they would inevitably have to ban IUDs and birth control pills since they also destroy life that has been conceived.[4]

Planned Parenthood, an organization committed to providing birth control to teenagers, has taken out full-page ads in major newspapers claiming that pro-lifers will not stop at banning surgical abortions but will inevitably want to ban the Pill because of its occasional abortifacient function.

Norplant

Evidence is growing that the new, long-term contraceptive implant may also have abortifacient properties. Though its principal means of operation is to prevent ovulation, research also shows that it inhibits sperm transport by altering the cervical mucous and alters the lining of the uterus.[5]

Research also demonstrates that Norplant is not 100 percent effective in preventing conception. Recently, researchers have concluded that Norplant users have a cumulative pregnancy rate at five years of 2.6 per 100 women.[6]

Spermicides

Spermicides do not appear to disrupt the fertilized egg; thus they do not appear to be abortifacients. However, one factor to consider before choosing this contraceptive is the association between spermicides and birth defects. Some researchers believe that spermicide does not always kill the sperm but, in some cases, damages it. A damaged sperm that fertilizes an egg could result in birth defects.

Sterilization

Where does a healthy couple in their twenties get the notion that after having two children without medical complication they should be permanently sterilized? It is hard to find biblical justification for permanent sterilization when no compelling medical or health reasons exist.

Some argue that emotional health is as valid a reason for preventing conception as physical health. However, I believe emotional health can be restored more quickly than physical health. A couple may believe they are not emotionally prepared to raise another child, only to change their minds a few years later. At one time or another all of us have dealt with situations we never thought we'd be able to handle. And circumstances may change, too. By permanently closing the door to more children, we may find ourselves with regrets.

Currently there is a trend among Christians to seek sterilization reversals. Growing numbers of Christian couples are willing to undergo this expensive medical procedure because they have concluded that they wrongly assumed too much control over their God-given procreative abilities. Others cannot afford a reversal but regret taking a permanent step to preclude additional children. Their experience should serve as a caution.

Natural Family Planning

Many who oppose or are uncomfortable with artificial means of conception control practice natural family planning, a method of monitoring the wife's menstrual cycle and signs of fertility. During peak fertility periods they abstain from sexual relations.

Whereas some argue that that is not conception control but a means of spacing children, it is difficult to assert that this does not include conception prevention, even though the means of prevention is abstinence. Couples that choose this method should acknowledge that it is a form of conception control.

Some refer to the Levitical ceremonial laws governing marital sexual relations following the woman's menstrual cycle or after the birth of a child as evidence of the Bible's support for natural family planning. However, the primary purpose of Old Testament references to abstaining from sexual relations following the birth of a child or the woman's menstrual period seems to be ceremonial cleanliness, not the numbering and spacing of children.

Natural family planning is a method that nearly any couple can use if they are willing to make the necessary commitment to monitoring the wife's ovulatory cycle and the personal discipline necessary to make it effective, such as abstinence during peak fertility periods.

Barrier Methods of Contraceptives

Condoms, sponges, and diaphragms represent, for the most part, nonchemical methods of preventing conception. However, they have a high "failure rate" (20 percent) as compared with other forms of conception control.

WHAT ABOUT CONCEPTION CONTROL FOR HEALTH REASONS?

Is it wrong for a couple to use conception control or permanent sterilization because of poor health? It is not unusual for a physician to advise a woman to avoid pregnancy when she has had difficult pregnancies or underlying health problems such as diabetes, which could be further exacerbated by a pregnancy. In such circumstances common sense dictates that pregnancy should be avoided. However, it is difficult to predict how seriously a woman's health will be affected by a term pregnancy, even if her health was good before conception. Predicting the impact of a pregnancy upon a woman in poor health is not a precise science either. High-risk pregnancy specialists recognize the limitations of their prognostic abilities, although studies of specific high-risk populations provide a general idea of how a particular woman may be affected. Even with the best data available, there are always women who beat the odds and make the "experts" look silly.

Yet maternal mortality and morbidity is a serious matter and should not be easily dismissed. Generally speaking, if the best information available to a physician indicates that a particular woman would be well advised to avoid pregnancy then such counsel should be heeded. If she has temporary medical complications that are correctable or will heal with time, using a temporary form of conception control in order to permit the body to heal may be appropriate. Using sterilization may be justified in instances where she has a significant lifelong medical problem that would be exacerbated by pregnancy.

If physical health is a valid reason for using conception control, shouldn't we recognize the importance of a woman's emotional health as well? Isn't emotional well-being as important as physical well-being?

Of course emotional health is vital, yet it is much more difficult to assess than physical health. What is emotional well-being? When a person says, "I just can't handle more than two children," is she saying that a third would push her over the edge into psychosis?

45

Some people claim, "I only have enough love for two children." But such a statement reduces love to a measurable commodity. Is love like money—finite and tangible? Sometimes couples who thought they had completed their families are blessed with a child later in life. Often these children bring more joy than imaginable. Although money may be in short supply, the parents usually seem to find enough love to go around.

THE EDUCATIONAL EFFECTS OF BIRTH CONTROL

Birth control has revolutionized the way we think about family, children, parenting, sex, and stewardship. The availability of contraceptive and birth control devices has been a major contributor to the sexual revolution, the results of which we are just beginning to comprehend. Of course, anything legitimate (television, printing) can be abused. Unfortunately, the church has not stopped to consider the abuse of conception control nor the effects of that abuse. Among the consequences:

- Churches are dealing with increasing numbers of "sexually active" teens in their congregations.
- Christian schools are being asked by public health officials to present students with material on "safe sex."
- Crisis pregnancy centers report surprising numbers of professing Christian women coming to them hoping to obtain abortions.
- Planned Parenthood, the nation's largest abortion provider, jokes about the number of Christian women they abort each year. Undoubtedly many Christian teens go to them for contraceptives as well.
- Christian parents agree to let their daughters use birth control pills, assuming that that is be better than risking an unwanted pregnancy.

Many Christians defend their use of contraception, saying that it strengthens their marriages and families. That was one of the principal arguments used in the legalization of the Pill, although the primary argument for legalizing contraceptives was the "right to privacy." Yet if contraception truly promoted marital harmony, control of fertility should have had a positive effect on family life. So how has the family faired since 1960, when the Pill came on the scene? Not well. Marriages do not last longer, and relationships between men and women have not improved in sensitivity and understanding. More, rather than less, sexual exploitation occurs today. There are more sexual assaults on women today, not fewer. Children are more likely to spend part of their childhood years in a single-parent home than before contraceptives were introduced. "Every child a wanted child" makes for a nice slogan, but society appears to be as far from achieving that goal as ever.

Child abuse of every kind is on the rise. Divorce racks the church as well as the secular world. Where are all those happy, healthy families that would improve social and economic conditions in our culture? Evidently the social planners and birth controllers promised something they couldn't deliver. In contrast, God says that happiness comes to the man who has his quiver full of children (Psalm 127:5).

I readily concede that other influences within Western culture have contributed to the demise of marriage and family. Conception control cannot be portrayed as the only cause. More than a few may even resist the idea that conception control is a cause at all.

However, when one looks closely at the underpinnings of the feminist and gay rights movements it is difficult to support that argument. Both groups have staked their claims on the right to privacy and reproductive freedom. Without a right to privacy that protects all sexual behavior among "consenting" individuals (and reliable artificial means of conception control to prevent the natural "consequences," that is, unwelcome children), the hopes of behavior-based "freedom to choose" groups would be dashed.

WHAT DOES THE BIBLE SAY?

Biblicists insist on testing every idea with Scripture. That is as it should be. Let us look at what the Bible has to say about children, motherhood, and human sexuality.

1. God commands us to be fruitful and multiply (Genesis 1:28).

That so-called "cultural mandate" remains in effect. The command was not restricted to Adam and Noah. Procreation was an important part of God's promises to Abraham, Moses, and David. Throughout the Old Testament there is an unmistakable emphasis on the blessing of children (Psalm 113:9; 127:3-5). The command to procreate applies to every generation. No single generation could fulfill it, just as no single generation could fulfill the Great Commission.

2. Fertility is a central feature of God's redemptive plan in both the Old and New Testaments.

It was through human childbirth that the Lord Jesus came to earth and became the propitiation for man's sin (1 John 2:1-2). Paul admonished young widows to remarry, have children, and keep their homes (1 Timothy 5:14). The blessing of fertility is exhibited in the lives of Sarah, Rachel, Hannah, and Elizabeth (Genesis 21:1-2; 30:22-24; 1 Samuel 1:11; Luke 1:24-25). Motherhood is esteemed within the pages of Scripture.

3. The Bible is pro-child.

Psalm 127:3-5 clearly expresses God's positive view of children: "Behold, children are a gift of the Lord; the fruit of the womb is a reward. Like arrows in the hand of a warrior, so are the children of one's youth. How blessed is the man whose quiver is full of them; they shall not be ashamed, when they speak with their enemies in the gate."

Children were considered a symbol of blessing. From Genesis to Malachi, the seed motif forms a dominant part of God's relationship with Israel. A central theme is the responsibility of God's children to raise up godly seed to follow the Lord's commands and enjoy His blessing. Malachi ends the Old Testament on that note. The New Testament takes up the theme as Jesus consistently demonstrates special treatment for children, blessing them and using them as illustrations of spiritual truth.

4. Believers are called to a life of faith (Habbakuk 2:4) and fidelity to all the teaching of Scripture.

Inasmuch as we profess belief in the God who is omnipotent, omniscient, omnipresent, and immutable, trusting Him should not be problematic. But it is. Although we have little trouble trusting our employer for a paycheck, on whose promise we signed up for a thirty-year mortgage, we are not as eager to trust God when it comes to the number and spacing of our children.

What happens when a Christian couples' birth control fails? Do they then consider abortion as a solution? Do they release the child for adoption? Place him or her in foster care? Hopefully they turn to the Lord to supply their needs, to give them the grace to handle another child.

I often hear couples say that if God wants them to have a child He will overcome their birth control. Could the opposite be true—that if God doesn't want them to have a child He will prevent conception?

In general, I believe that God wants us to want children in whatever number He gives. Playing semantic games and using arguments from ignorance is a poor way to deal with the privilege of bringing divine image bearers into this world.

I hasten to add that bringing children into this world is not the end of our responsibility. Parents are also responsible to care for their children's spiritual, physical, emotional, and educational needs. In short, parents are to help their children become responsible adults. Unfortunately, many seem to think that that cannot be accomplished unless a child has his own room and a college tuition annuity plan. Our perception of what constitutes an acceptable standard of living not only distorts the values our children are learning but also prevents many couples from having children at all.

Jesus taught that we should be happy knowing that our Father in heaven knows our physical needs (Matthew 6:25-32). Likewise, Paul admonished believers to learn to be content, whether they have little or much (Hebrews 13:5). Faith means trusting God in every circumstance.

5. Human beings do not reproduce—they procreate.

Man is not just a part of nature; he is above nature. Being made in God's image means that man is not just a higher form of animal life. Man is more than a "speck of mind in a mindless universe."

God places a high value on marriage and the one-flesh relationship. Marriage is for a lifetime, and the sexuality expressed in marriage is intended to facilitate an intimacy that deepens the love and affection the partners feel for one another in order to represent the way Christ loves His church.

The Bible does not teach mindless reproduction, whereby men and women regularly turn out litters of children. Scripture teaches parenting—a shepherding, training, and nurturing of young image bearers (Deuteronomy 6:4-9; Ephesians 6:1-4). Effective, godly parenting is a requirement for those aspiring to the office of pastor and deacon. Paul indicates that that is not incidental to spiritual leadership but a manifestation of spiritual leadership (1 Timothy 3:4-5).

Procreation is like evangelism in that both are a divine-human cooperative. In evangelism we are the instrument through which the gospel is proclaimed to others, but it is God the Holy Spirit who brings about regeneration. We present the gospel many times when regeneration does not occur, and physical procreation is similar. A husband and wife engage in sexual relations with the possibility of procreation occurring. There is no guarantee that it will, just as there is no guarantee that spiritual procreation will occur whenever we communicate the gospel.

I believe that just as God is involved in the supernatural work of spiritual procreation, He is also involved in physical procreation. My youngest daughter asked me recently, "Daddy, if you never met Mommy, where would I be right now?" I answered, "Emily, you wouldn't exist if Mommy and I had never met." In fact, if my wife and I had had sexual relations at a different time the biological fact is that Emily would not be here. That is a great mystery to me, but I believe God wanted us to have an Emily Anne instead of an Adam Paul. If conception had taken place a month earlier or a month later we may have had a girl whom we named "Emily." However, she would not be the Emily we know and love. She is a once-in-a-lifetime girl, as is every child, because a different ovum and a different sperm cell would have resulted in a person different from Emily.

That is what makes procreation special and places it in a category unlike other biological processes. That is why we must be extremely careful not to presume absolute control over it. Bearing children is more than a physiological function. To bring a child into this world involves both human and divine instrumentation. It is a serious business.

Conceptions resulting from rape, incest, or other tragic and exceptional circumstances present us with a dilemma. Many consider such children to be less valuable (more expendable) than those born into loving, two-parent homes. Such views spring from the peculiar idea that a child conceived outside of God's ideal of marriage cannot serve a purpose in God's overall plan. One only needs to look at biblical history to disprove that assumption. The lineage of Christ includes people conceived under less than ideal circumstances. Judah slept with his daughter-in-law, Tamar, thinking she was a prostitute (Genesis 38:11-30). Obviously, both were involved in sin. Yet from the union came twin boys, Perez and Zerah, ancestors of David and, ultimately, of the Lord Jesus Christ Himself. Although God does not bless rape, incest, or adultery, He can bring good out of the worst circumstances. If we learn anything from the Bible it should be that God specializes in taking people wrecked by sin and turning them into trophies of His grace.

As I have already stated, I do not believe sex is strictly for procreative purposes. First Corinthians 7 and other passages attest to the fact that God designed the expression of sexuality in marriage as a means of deepening intimacy, enhancing the one-flesh relationship, promoting communication, and procreating children.

Conservative Christians are typically concerned with the appearance of evil as much as with evil itself, citing Paul's admonition to "abstain from all appearance of evil" (1 Thessalonians 5:22, KJV). Thus it is difficult to understand how artificial conception control has gained such a foothold among conservative Christians. Perhaps we should exercise greater caution in adopting a lifestyle that incorporates practices whose origins are theologically suspect. How can a faith community that takes the Bible seriously and is concerned with avoiding every appearance of evil embrace a practice whose beginnings are connected to people hostile to all that Christianity stands for? Why are we so uncritical of the origins of birth control when we are so meticulous in other areas to avoid giving credibility to those who mock and despise our God?

The practice of birth control emerged from a movement that was and still is openly hostile to Christianity. Margaret Sanger, one of the most prominent birth control pioneers, made no secret of her disapproval of anyone who held conservative religious convictions. Sanger's organization, Planned Parenthood, continues her legacy of trying to tear down the Judeo-Christian view of morality. Like Sanger, Planned Parenthood has adopted a view of sexuality not rooted in Scripture. In fact, in most instances its philosophy is diametrically opposed to Scripture.[7]

If you read the lives of birth control pioneers such as Margaret Sanger, Francis Place, Richard Carlile, Robert Dale Owen, Charles Knowlton, and others, you will find that every one of them lived far from God. Some were involved in the occult and led immoral lives. Are these examples for us to emulate? Paul admonishes believers to imitate God (Ephesians 5:1) and also tells us not to be conformed to the world system (Romans 12:1-2).

Consider the most vocal advocates of birth control in our own day. In nearly every case they promote abortion, sexual perversion, and other practices that destroy the family. Eleanor Smeal, former president of the National Organization for Women and current president of the Fund for the Feminist Majority, argues that birth control is the foundation upon which women's rights are built. She has been a consistent and vocal advocate for expanding abortion rights. The current president of NOW, Patricia Ireland, recently acknowledged that she has a lesbian lover. Ireland is also an outspoken proponent of abortion and gay rights. Similar views are expressed by

Molly Yard (NOW), Kate Michelman (National Abortion Rights Action League), and Faye Wattleton (former president of the Planned Parenthood Federation of America). The connection of these names to birth control alone should cause Christians to stop and reconsider. How can birth control be at the same time the bedrock of the feminist movement and an accepted practice among Bible-believing Christians?

I realize that that is an extreme statement and that some readers will consider me extreme for linking pro-abortion feminists with Bible-believing Christians. One might argue that there are many inventions, drugs, and commodities that we. all use and whose inventors or manufacturers were not believers. Why should birth control be placed under suspicion simply because of the character of those who advocate it?

Unlike automobiles, television, radio, or other products, the aim of birth control is to prevent or eliminate human lives. Second, the only way birth control became legal was through a tearing away at the Judeo-Christian roots of our legal system and our family values. Therefore, Christians need to think seriously about accepting a practice that was introduced as a means of circumventing the consequences of ignoring biblical standards for marriage and family. As Jesus asked, "Grapes are not gathered from thorn bushes, nor figs from thistles, are they?" (Matthew 7:16). Christians would be wise to read some of the books written by the early advocates of birth control. Read Margaret Sanger's *Pivot of Civilization* or *The New Motherhood.* You will discover that Sanger was quite aware of the Christian community's opposition to her teachings. Her lifestyle was definitely not an example for a Christian to imitate.

Concern for the environment, fear of overpopulation, or other social catastrophes are not what motivate most people to control their fertility today. The few studies that focus on what motivates people to use conception control on a regular basis reveal that personal interests such as economics, emotional stability, and careers are principal motivators.

Christians are as likely to use conception control as nonbelievers, and there is little difference in the motivation of the two groups. In fact, women seeking abortions frequently do so for the same reasons that believers use conception control. Clearly conception control is much different from aborting a child, but we cannot ignore the fact that the motivation in both instances is frequently the same.

Control over one's fertility has become institutionalized in our society. It is considered by the medical community, special interest groups, feminists, population organizations, federal and state government, and international aid organizations to be a major part of national and international public policy. Those who obtain abortions are willing to carry that control to the furthest degree. But the Christian who blindly uses conception control is also exerting a degree of control over her fertility.

It may appear that I am totally against Christians using conception control. Yet I must confess that the matter is not completely resolved for me. What has been resolved in my own mind is that the indiscriminate use of conception control by Christians is a serious problem. It has infected our youth with unbiblical and unhealthy views of marriage and family. Fewer and fewer Christian youth see children as blessings from God. I am concerned about the attitudes young people express toward parenting. The decline is evidenced when one hears Christian college students talk about how few children they plan to have. Negative attitudes toward children are on the increase, perhaps fueled by parents who complain about how expensive children are, sowing in their offsprings' spirits a carnal and unbiblical attitude toward children. What happens in the average church when a woman in her late thirties becomes pregnant with her fourth or fifth child? Do people admire her? Usually she hears such things as, "Haven't you ever heard of birth control?" or, "Was this a planned pregnancy?" or, "I'm glad it's you and not me!" Whereas some comments are made in jest, many are not.

What we do teaches. Children observe the actions and attitudes of adults, especially their parents. The modern "take charge" approach that has become the norm among believers has not gone unnoticed by today's Christian youth. It is not difficult to figure out where young people get their negative attitudes about marriage and family. Although that attitude is not found in every Christian family, it is not unusual. Perhaps that explains why Christian young people delay marriage and struggle with personal relationships as much as their secular counterparts—and why growing numbers of Christian youth have adopted a recreational view of sex.

It is not unusual for churches to discriminate against missionaries with large families, even to the point of denying support for those with more than four children. On more than a few occasions missionaries have asked me if it could be God's will for them to forsake missions when the wife became pregnant with number five. Pastors and missions boards routinely advise missionaries to limit the size of their family because churches are reluctant to support large families. I have even been rebuked by church members for having four children, suggesting that it is wrong when my financial support comes from local churches.

Before we criticize missionaries with large families we should consider where many missionaries come from. It should come as no surprise—from missionary families. We should praise the Lord for missionaries who fulfill the Great Commission with their children. How many people in this world might be without a gospel witness if missionaries didn't have children and rear them to serve the Lord? I believe the wise church invests in missionaries who have large families.

Although an explicit biblical warning against the use of artificial conception control does not exist, the Bible is far more pro-child and pro-parenting than we might think. And Christians would be wiser to take their cues from Scripture than from secular culture. Perhaps we need to reexamine our attitudes in order to be certain that we are in line with Scripture and God's will.

CHRISTIAN PHYSICIANS
AND SINGLE FEMALE PATIENTS

Christian physicians are frequently asked for prescriptions for conception control by single women. Such requests place the doctor in a bind. He must either violate his conscience by facilitating illicit sexual behavior or live with the possibility that she will become pregnant and abort.

Several factors must be considered here. First, the Christian physician must determine which comes first in his life—his faith or his medical practice. Should he approach his patients purely from a medical perspective or does he treat them from a biblical perspective as well?

If the Christian doctor prescribes contraceptives without warning his patient of the potential dangers she faces—physically, emotionally, and spiritually—he does her a disservice. It is not good medical practice to withhold from a patient information that could be useful in avoiding further injury or harm. That violates the principle of nonmaleficence. If a physician prescribes contraceptives for a single woman without warning her of the consequences, then that physician has done her a disservice, both medically and morally.

In our sin-drenched culture, just mentioning abstinence brings accusations of "ramming morality down people's throats." Yet God calls His children to maintain His standards of morality before a generation that has abandoned those standards. The Christian physician is in a unique position to be God's mouthpiece in a way a pastor can be.

If a father brings his fourteen-year-old daughter to a Christian physician saying he wants a prescription for birth control pills for her since they are having sexual relations, would the doctor be imposing his morality on him by refusing to comply? Most would agree that compliance would facilitate incest, which is not only immoral but illegal. Is facilitating fornication less immoral? Is God less indignant about premarital sex than about incest?

Providing contraceptives to a single woman indicates a decision to treat her as merely a physical being and ignores the fact that she is also a spiritual being. A medical "solution" is no panacea for what is essentially a moral problem. Although contraception may protect her from pregnancy, it does not protect her from the injury to her spirit that illicit sexual activity will inevitably cause. The Christian physician who refuses to comply with that request does her a favor. She may reject his counsel and obtain contraceptives from someone else, but at least she did not receive the impression that a Christian condoned her behavior.

Some Christian physicians prescribe contraceptives for single women because the women threaten that they will obtain an abortion if they become pregnant. But that threat is only a smoke screen. People threaten physicians with all kinds of things. The threat of an immoral act is no justification for committing another immoral act. And the patient is responsible for her own actions, as the physician is for his.

CONCLUSION

I am deeply troubled by the fact that conception control is practiced by many Christians without careful and prayerful consideration. I know couples who spend a considerable amount of time praying about the purchase of a home but admit that they never prayed about using birth control or the number of children God wants them to have. I am more concerned with our prayerlessness on this issue than I am with the actual use of conception control devices. Shouldn't we be a people who approach God about our children? A question of this magnitude must warrant a season of careful and prayerful consideration before the Lord.

As I stated at the beginning of the chapter, it is not my role to play the Holy Spirit and determine God's will for every Christian. In general, I believe a healthy husband and wife should be open to the possibility of children in their lives. In intimating God (Ephesians 5:1) we could argue that just as God created the universe according to a conscious plan, we should procreate according to a conscious plan. Perhaps temporary circumstances may justify avoiding conception and childbearing. However, we should exercise great care in making decisions about permanent sterilization. We should be open to the fact that God has the right to change our plan.

Marriage involves both commitment and sacrifice. In taking marriage vows we are making a commitment to God, to our mate, and to the unknown. None of us can predict our future. We may do our best as conscious image bearers to plan for it, but there are no guarantees. One thing we can know, however, is that God can be trusted. He invites us to cast all of our concerns and cares upon Him, because He not only cares but possesses the ability to meet our needs (1 Peter 5:7). I believe that extends to the question of how large a family God wants us to have. If the grace of God is sufficient for the ill, the disabled, and the persecuted, then we must believe it is sufficient for those whom God has blessed with many children.

QUESTIONS TO THINK ABOUT

1. What are some reasons for limiting family size? Are they valid?
2. Upon what biblical basis can we justify the use of conception control for both Christians and non-Christians?
3. What biblical reasons can be given to oppose conception control?
4. What are some valid criteria for determining family size?
5. What should a Christian physician do when asked to provide contraceptives for an unmarried woman?

4

FETAL EXPERIMENTATION

Is was only a matter of time before enterprising capitalists discovered ways to make money from abortion even after it was over. Japanese Buddhist temples rake in $350 million a year selling stone statues to women who have had abortions. An accompanying elaborate ceremony is meant to quell the troubled spirits of the dead children and ease the consciences of the mothers. Beyond the millions being made by abortionists, medical researchers in the West have found a more sophisticated way to commercialize the "products of conception"—fetal experimentation.

FETAL TISSUE TRANSPLANTS

In 1987, Dr. Curtis Freed, a researcher at the University of Colorado Health Sciences Center, transplanted cells from an aborted baby into the brain of a Parkinson's patient, hoping to reverse the destructive effects of the disease. Similar procedures have been performed in Mexico, Sweden, Spain, Great Britain, Cuba, and, reportedly, China.

In early 1988, the National Institutes of Health, under orders from the Secretary of Health and Human Services, placed a moratorium on federal funding of fetal tissue research until an advisory panel could report on the ethical issues involved. During the moratorium, researchers were free to continue their experiments as long as they were funded privately.

In 1990, the advisory panel reported its findings and recommended that the moratorium be lifted, claiming that the research held significant promise for treating not only Parkinson's disease but also Alzheimers, diabetes, and other ailments. The benefits supposedly outweighed the liabilities, so it was recommended that funding be provided from the federal treasury. On February 5, 1992, the Senate Labor and Human Resources Committee approved (13-4) a measure to lift the ban on federal funding of fetal tissue transplantation research. The bill overwhelmingly passed in the full Senate and in the U.S. House of Representatives in May 1992, with only a presidential veto standing in the way of its becoming law.

Proponents of fetal tissue research argue that the issue of where the tissue comes from is secondary to whether others benefit from it. Traditionally pro-life legislators, such as Senators Robert Dole (R–Kansas) and Strom Thurmond (R–South Carolina), supported efforts to lift the ban on federal funding for fetal tissue research. They claim that this "is a pro-life position." But is it? Are there not profound moral and ethical problems involved with harvesting tissues from babies whose lives are deemed inconvenient and insignificant?

Proponents of fetal tissue research argue that obtaining tissue from convenience abortions does not mean that we condone or endorse the morality of abortion any more than using the organs of homicide victims condones murder. They insist that a line can be drawn between the immorality of abortion and the morality of using tissues obtained from those abortions.

They also focus on the benefits of using tissue that would otherwise be wasted. A frequently asked question is: Why should perfectly good tissue be flushed down the sewer system when it could help people live? In our environmentally-aware culture, it makes sense to recycle human tissues to benefit society.

James Burtchaell of the University of Notre Dame cautions, "Whatever motivates these pleas, they are the echoes of Nuremburg,"[1] in reference to the Nuremburg Tribunals at which Nazi doctors attempted to justify their experiments on

Jewish prisoners as moral since their subjects were going to die anyway by execution.

Can fetal tissue research be morally justified within a sanctity of life ethic? No, for several reasons.

First, the use of fetal tissue from elective abortions is not the same as using the organs from a murder victim. The physician who removes organs from a murder victim does not make a plan, saying, "Today I will harvest organs from murder victims." Murder is unplanned as far as the physicians harvesting and transplanting the organs are concerned.

In fetal tissue research that is not the case. Although researchers may not know that a particular abortion will be performed on a particular day, their workday is premised on the knowledge that someone will be killing unborn babies.

Dr. Freed's experiment, for example, involved going to the abortion clinic with his own containers, witnessing the abortion to make sure the procedure did as little damage to the tissue as possible (ignoring the fact that a baby was killed), and personally examining the remains in order to separate the brain tissue. He was an accessory to murder, much as a physician would be if he hired a hit man to kill a potential organ donor. No amount of humanitarian "good" can obscure the fact that Freed knew when, where, and how the homicide would take place.

Second, how can fetal tissue be referred to as "donated tissue" or "anatomical gifts" if the humanity of the unborn is denied? Only persons can donate. In fetal tissue donations, it is the mother who "donates" the tissue. But whose mother is it? Nonpersons don't have mothers. In fact, the tissue is desirable because it is human.

Third, cannibalizing the bodies of aborted babies pits the value of the born against the value of the unborn. Arguments for fetal tissue research suggest that using the tissue of human beings is a legitimate activity since sick people are helped. But how legitimate is it to cure one person who is ill by killing someone who is healthy?

Fourth, fetal tissue transplants further line the pockets of abortionists because they typically charge a "handling fee" of $25 to $50 per baby.

Fifth, fetal tissue transplants, if successful, could proliferate into a billion dollar business, resulting in women's conceiving with the intent of aborting children for medical purposes. Already women have conceived children for the purpose of providing bone marrow for another sibling. The media has reported on women who volunteer to conceive in order to produce compatible tissue for the treatment of a loved one's Alzheimers or their own diabetes.

Sadly, those babies are viewed as providing something in death that they could not provide in life. A preborn baby's brain cells purportedly contain the power to extend life for Alzheimers patients, but in life the same child's brain might have found the cure for the disease itself.

Fetal tissue transplants are a bad idea, even if they are medically beneficial, which has still not been conclusively demonstrated. They are a bad idea because they dehumanize the unborn, treating them as a collection of interchangeable parts. They also threaten to further dehumanize our thinking about human beings in general.

Victims of Parkinson's and other diseases deserve compassion and understanding. They deserve practical assistance and support and the best medical care possible. Medical research should focus on legitimate means of providing relief, such as the current research with L-dopa, which has been shown to relieve some symptoms of Parkinson's. The cure does not need to come from acts of violence against the healthy.

Abortion is morally bankrupt public policy in itself; trying to salve our national conscience by claiming that at least something good comes out of it does nothing to remove our moral culpability.

FETAL EXPERIMENTATION WITH
ABORTED BABIES AND EXCESS IVF EMBRYOS

In 1976 Turtox-Cambosco, a firm based in Chicago and a subsidiary of MacMillian Publishing Company, listed in its catalog "embedments of human embryos" for $97.80, with the description, "These embryos range from 3 to 4 months in age. They have been bisected along the median, cleared and mounted naturally. Specify age or ages desired."[2] On March 2, 1981, _The Arizona Republic_ reported that state officials investigated doctors affiliated with the Valley Abortion Center, who were reported to have been experimenting on human fetuses even though such experiments were prohibited by state law. A review of recent research literature reveals that fetal experimentation is not uncommon, even where it is illegal.

Much experimentation is made possible by in vitro fertilization because it involves a common practice of harvesting multiple ovum, fertilizing all of them and freezing those that are left over. In vitro fertilization (IVF) is presented as a way for physicians to assist women with blocked oviducts or fallopian tubes, preventing natural procreation. IVF appears to be a compassionate way to help such women realize their dream of bearing children.

An in-depth discussion of IVF is undertaken in chapter 5, so I will not go into all the details here. However, IVF, as it is currently practiced, often yields multiple ovum, which are inseminated and allowed to grow to a stage where they are suitable for transfer to the uterus. It is not unusual for an IVF clinic to cryo-preserve extra embryos, either to be used in another attempt if the current cycle fails to produce a term pregnancy, or to be donated to another couple.

The embryos can also be used in fetal experimentation. Some experimentation involves research to discover new genetic screening procedures, test various drugs and their effect on developing human beings, and so on.[3]

If you agree with the advocates of abortion that the unborn child is not a person, then the moral status of the preimplantation human embryo is of little consequence. It is not a person; therefore, using embryos is not unethical. That seems to be the majority view in the medical research community. They are not experimenting with living persons, and their goals are humanitarian.

However, the reason their experiments have any value is that they are experimenting with living human beings. The research may save some babies' lives, but at what cost?

The morality of human experimentation has been the subject of intense debate for decades. An incident that sparked considerable controversy and led to the passage of federal regulations to oversee human experimentation was the Tuskegee Syphilis Study. Black men from Alabama were infected with syphilis and deliberately not treated in order to study the long-term effects of the disease. The study ran for forty years, from 1932 until 1972, before it was revealed and halted.

Current regulations concerning research on human subjects are quite explicit; the subjects must be informed of the nature of the research and risks involved. However, pre-implantation human embryos cannot give informed consent. They cannot speak for themselves. Also, such experimentation is 100 percent fatal. None of those small human beings will ever see the light of day. The research will not benefit them at all.

Reality is often swallowed up by the rhetoric of humanitarianism. The public is cowed into believing that many lives are potentially saved by such research, but that defense focuses on the wrong issue. What is the cost in terms of human life? How many lives will be sacrificed in order for our research to be "conclusive"?

Traditional principles of medical ethics—autonomy, beneficence, nonmaleficence, justice—are twisted to fit this situation. The loser is not only the unborn. Society in general is further dehumanized. Whereas the research is presented as being conducted under the most impeccable humanitarian auspices, the reality is that we are devaluing some human beings in order to demonstrate how much value we place on others. Saul Bellow wrote,

> Everything in modern times is done brutally and in haste and processed quickly. We are divested of the deeper human meaning that has traditionally been attached to human life. . . . There is no sacred space around human beings any more. It's not necessary to approach them with the tentativeness and respect that civilization has always accorded them. People are now out there in the open; they're fair game. . . . Our humanity is at risk. It's too powerful a thing to just lie down and

give up the ghost. But we have to face the fact that it is in danger. It is at risk because the feeling that life is sacred has died away in this century.[4]

QUESTIONS TO THINK ABOUT

1. When does individual personal existence begin?
2. How would you define "personhood"?
3. What is the moral status of the pre-implantation human embryo?
4. Is it wrong for a Christian to receive medical benefit from a procedure or drug made possible by experimenting with living human embryos?

5

INFERTILITY AND MEDICALLY ASSISTED PROCREATION

For centuries embarrassed parents have been vexed by the child's query, "Where do babies come from?" Until recently, one didn't need a degree in reproductive endocrinology to answer this question—just courage.

Today, however, babies come from an ever-widening variety of sources: natural procreation, in vitro fertilization, gamete intra-fallopian transfer, low-tubal ovum transfer, zygote intra-fallopian transfer, uterine lavage, artificial insemination by the husband, artificial insemination by donor, surrogate mothering, or other methods developed since the writing of this book.

The boom in medically assisted procreation techniques has been prompted by the combination of need (a growing number of infertile couples), changing moral values concerning the unborn child, and the development of sophisticated reproductive technologies.

For the last seven of their ten years of marriage, Jack and Susan* have been trying to have a baby, spending more than $35,000 in their quest. Adding injury to insult, Susan has undergone numerous tests and painful physical examinations and procedures, while fending off the all too frequent question, "When are you two finally going to settle down and have children?"

* Fictitious names have been used.

The most disappointing aspect of the ordeal is that after spending so much money and enduring so much pain, the doctors have diagnosed Jack and Susan's condition as "unexplained infertility."

Jack and Susan are not alone. Currently, well more than 2 million couples experience infertility.[1] Generally, infertility is defined as a couple's inability to conceive after twelve months of regular intercourse without contraception. Nearly one out of every four women experiences a fertility problem.

SOURCES OF INFERTILITY

The three most common contributors to female infertility are problems with ovulation (amenorrhea), blocked or scarred fallopian tubes, and endometriosis (the presence of scar tissue on the uterine wall or endometrial cavity). Roughly 50 percent of women who undergo conventional infertility treatment (hormone therapy, surgery, and so on) are helped. However, that leaves 50 percent whose condition remains unchanged.

According to the National Centers for Disease Control, sexually transmitted diseases (STDs) account for more than 20 percent of infertility.[2] Pelvic inflammatory disease (PID), which is common to women with sexually transmitted diseases, often damages ovaries, fallopian tubes, and the lining of the uterus. That is particularly tragic since STDs are preventable.

Chlamydia trachomatis infects 4 million people annually, mostly teenage girls (nearly 50 percent of all PID cases involve a teenage girl with chlamydia). It is not unusual for a woman to have more than one PID episode, which dramatically increases her chances of infertility. Tragically, many infected women do not discover their disease until their late twenties or early thirties when they begin to think about starting a family. PID is a vivid reminder that much of the pain of infertility can be avoided if people follow biblical principles of sexuality.

Infertility is not always behavior based. Other known causes of infertility are regular, vigorous physical exercise, genetic factors, environmental toxins, and birth defects. Regardless of the cause, the emotional pain of infertility is real.

67

THE TECHNOLOGY AND MORALITY
OF MEDICALLY ASSISTED PROCREATION

The medical community has been motivated to find a remedy for childlessness. Whereas relatively few new treatments have been developed for infertility itself, a number of new technologies have been developed to assist infertile couples in their quest for a biological child.

Artificial Insemination

Artificial insemination (AI) is the oldest and least complicated of the assisted procreation techniques. Historians believe artificial insemination was first used with humans in 1792.[3] AI is often used when the husband has a low sperm count, seminal vesicle dysfunction, or ejaculatory duct blockage. In general, AI has a high success rate, compared to other forms of medically assisted procreation. Currently, several hundred thousand people are alive who were conceived by artificial insemination.

Artificial insemination takes two forms: AIH uses sperm from the husband, and AID uses sperm from an anonymous donor. Sperm is obtained by masturbation or by medical means, if the man has moral objections to masturbation. It is also possible for the couple to collect sperm in a condom during intercourse.

Virtually all AI programs utilize sperm preparation in which the sperm are washed to separate sperm cells from blood or antibodies contained in the semen. The process serves to concentrate the healthy sperm cells. A "swim up" process is utilized to concentrate the most motile sperm for the insemination process, usually facilitated by layering a solution containing proteins or other substances over the semen. Motility, the ability to move spontaneously, increases the likelihood of fertilization. The most motile sperm swim to the top of the solution, leaving behind most of the abnormal and nonmotile sperm.

Once prepared, the sperm are placed near the cervical canal or into the uterus itself by syringe or catheter. Some physicians use multiple inseminations to increase the possibility of fertilization. Intra-uterine insemination is performed most often in cases where it is known that the woman's cervical mucus is hostile to sperm cells. All AI techniques attempt insemination as near the date of female ovulation as possible. The timing is usually determined indirectly by checking the woman's basal body temperature.

AI can also use the sperm of a donor. Sperm banks have existed for at least twenty years, although the last ten years has seen a dramatic increase in the use of donated sperm. The use of donated sperm provokes the most significant moral controversy, although many are equally uncomfortable with AIH.

Some arguments against artificial insemination. Perhaps the most common argument against AI is that it is not natural, that it falls outside the bounds of natural procreation. Some argue that the natural order is a revelation of God's moral character; therefore, to interfere with it is to interfere with God's moral character, or at least His providential involvement in this world. Bioethicist Leon Kass asks, "Is there possibly some wisdom in that mystery of nature which joins the pleasure of sex, the communication of love and the desire for children in the very activity by which we continue the chain of human existence?"[4]

A second argument advanced against AI is that it introduces a third party into the procreative relationship—in fact several third parties if one uses a fertility clinic. Those who hold this view contend that God designed marriage to involve sexual intimacy between the husband and his wife alone, not other people.

Third, AI reduces procreation to a mechanical problem. It is believed that AI makes procreation too technical and scientific, removing the mystery and wonder from the start of a human life.

A fourth argument involves objections to masturbation. Some believe that masturbation violates biblical commands against fornication. However, that problem can be avoided by retrieving sperm via medical means rather than masturbation. Also, the distinction has been made between masturbation for self-gratification and masturbation for the purpose of procreation.

Fifth, AI is sometimes abused by lesbians. For example, a lesbian Episcopal priest invited three male friends to her home to masturbate so that she could mix the sperm and inseminate herself. She told a national television audience that she wanted the child to develop close bonds with no one but herself. The *Washington Post* described her as the "first artificially inseminated priest in the world,"[5] which is no doubt true. However, it is important to remember that the abuse of a technology does not render the technology itself immoral.

A sixth argument is that medically assisted procreation violates the sovereignty of God. Some Christians believe that God is directly involved in every conception, which means that He is also directly involved in each instance where conception does not occur. God opens and closes the womb by direct causation, and to interfere is to "play God."

However, it is difficult to maintain a consistent application of direct causation without addressing circumstances that clearly are not the design of a holy God. Are we prepared to argue that God directly causes rape and incest? Does God cause men and women to commit adultery?

Christians and artificial insemination. Bizarre use aside, should a Christian ever employ AI? Is it morally permissible for a Christian couple to use sperm from a donor, or should Christians avoid technology, believing that God has complete control of their procreative abilities? Is it "unnatural" to use AI? In one sense, AI is simply a logical progression of society's efforts to control human sexuality. Noncoital procreation is the logical extension of the conception control mentality.

In a society that already has difficulty remembering the relationship between human sexuality and marital commitment, exposing procreation to the clinician's expertise may be inviting additional harm.

AI is unnatural in the sense that most babies are not conceived that way. Yet, if we argue that Christian should not use anything unnatural, we may arrive at some peculiar conclusions. What would you call giving sight to the blind, restoring the dead to life, healing the deaf, and enabling the crippled to walk? The Lord Jesus Christ did all those things, and we call it supernatural. It was unnatural—and supernatural.

Few Christians object to medical interventions in "nature" to treat cancer, tuberculosis, appendicitis, and a host of other physical problems. Is it unnatural to freshen breath artificially, clip fingernails, or trim hair? Is it unnatural to fly an airplane, ride in a car, or watch television? On its own, the unnatural argument does not present a compelling case against artificial insemination.

The second argument is more convincing—using donor sperm introduces a third party into the procreative relationship. Serious moral questions must be answered concerning the introduction of third parties into this most private and intimate relationship. Sexual intimacy and procreation constitute an important part of the "one flesh" relationship between a husband and wife. Allowing a third party to manipulate procreative gametes removes the intimacy from the procreative process and reduces it to something observable by microscope. When a donor provides the sperm for insemination, a further disruption of the unitive aspect of marriage occurs. Of course, if the couple is infertile there is no procreation occurring on any level—intimate or otherwise.

Currently, an estimated 250,000 children in the U.S. have been conceived through AID, and the number is rising. The use of sperm and egg donors is increasing. AID is the most common form of third party birthing arrangement. Most, if not all, sperm banks operate on the basis of anonymity in order to protect the identity of the donors, while classifying sperm by race, height, hair and eye color, and IQ.

Some question whether AID is a form of adultery. But no illicit sexual relationship exists between the woman and the donor, and there is no intercourse, eliminating the possibility of sexual lust. The sperm are usually frozen for some time before the insemination process; therefore there is scarce possibility of contact between the donor and the woman. From the standpoint of physical interaction and direct communication between donor and woman, it does not appear that AID would constitute adultery.

However, one's procreative abilities are definitely part of the "one flesh" relationship spoken of in Genesis 2:24. Becoming one flesh means that the man and woman consent to a lifelong relationship with one another. Paul warned that a man should not take up with a prostitute since sexual intimacy is a vital part of the one-flesh relationship (1 Corinthians 6:16). Access to one's sexual/procreative powers is to be reserved for the person to whom a lifelong commitment is made. That aspect of a couple's relationship is so personal and intimate that the only thing that it can be likened to is Christ's relationship to His church.

In AID, the wife (with encouragement from her husband) submits her procreative powers to those of another man. Although she fulfills her procreative desires and potential, her husband does not. In that sense the unitive aspect of marriage has been harmed, which means that AID cannot be endorsed by Christians.

The fact that AID (as well as other forms of noncoital procreation) reduces procreation to a chemistry experiment also causes concern. Although that may not be a compelling argument in its own right, the medicalizing of procreation is morally problematic. Although AIH does not seem to have the moral baggage of AID, it, too, tends to medicalize the procreative process. However, that is not sufficiently compelling to rule out AIH as an option.

In Vitro Fertilization

In 1984, *People* magazine named Louise Brown one of the ten most prominent people of the decade, her claim to fame being the first live birth from in vitro fertilization (IVF).[6] A "test tube baby," Louise had her beginnings in a laboratory petri dish in Great Britain. Drs. Patrick Steptoe and Robert Edwards retrieved an egg from Louise's mother and sperm from her father, observed their union under a microscope, and subsequently transferred her embryonic form to her mother's uterus, where she developed to term.

Since her birth, more than 140 IVF clinics have sprung up in the U.S. Such clinics close the circle opened by the introduction of effective means of contraception. Now medical science can completely control the procreative process, whether the desire is to limit childbearing in fertile women or facilitate it in those who are infertile. Therefore, we now have sex without procreation and procreation without sex.

By 1989, more than 5,000 children were conceived outside the bodies of their mothers. This technology could be the next billion-dollar-per-year business in North America. Fertility and Genetics Research, Inc., a growing private company, estimates that as many as 50,000 women are eligible for embryo transfers each year, at a projected fee of $10,000 per procedure.[7]

IVF consists of four steps: ovarian hyperstimulation, ovum retrieval, insemination, and embryo transfer. Women who have blocked oviducts or fallopian tubes, which prevent eggs from being inseminated, most often choose IVF as a solution. By removing the eggs from the ovaries and inseminating them in a petri dish, conception can be achieved. Once conception occurs, the embryos can be transferred back into the woman's uterus, where hopefully a full-term pregnancy will develop. The overall success rate among U.S. clinics is about 11 percent, significantly lower than that of natural procreation.

The most compelling argument in favor of IVF is that homes have children in them that would not otherwise. How can you tell a couple that their child should not exist? How do you convince them that the procedure is not God's will when they hold in their arms a beautiful, healthy child?

Several factors must be considered when assessing the morality of IVF. First is the question of harvesting multiple ovum. Early IVF methods involved waiting for the woman to ovulate during her normal cycle. The retrieval team had to be prepared to do the laproscopy (a surgical procedure in which eggs are retrieved) at any time. The team would only harvest one ovum, which could prove to be unsuitable. Today most IVF clinics use a technique known as "ovarian hyperstimulation" in which follicular stimulation hormones are used to produce multiple ovum in a single ovulatory cycle.

Ovarian hyperstimulation allows clinicians to retrieve multiple ovum during regular business hours, making the retrieval process more manageable and increasing the potential for a successful pregnancy since more eggs can be fertilized and transferred into the mother's uterus. Ovarian hyperstimulation is cost effective since multiple eggs can be harvested at one time, thereby eliminating the need to repeat the procedure should one particular treatment cycle not yield a baby. Extra eggs can be frozen for use at a later time.

That presents several moral problems. One is that ovarian hyperstimulation goes beyond the imitation of natural procreation. Seldom does a woman produce as many as twelve ovum during one menstrual cycle. If our goal is to replicate nature, shouldn't we be satisfied with one egg, since God can superintend the fertilization of one egg just as well as several? Ovarian hyperstimulation pushes us beyond nature, albeit for the seemingly valid reasons of economics and time. However, if we are only trying to "help" nature along and not usurp the role of God, do we really need to harvest six to twelve ovum?

Due to hyperstimulation, a sizeable number of ovum are wasted. Even more significant is the loss of human embryos when multiple conceptions and transfers occur. Should we not have reservations about a process that significantly exceeds nature, particularly when the odds are that most embryos, if not all, will not survive? Some claim that the embryo loss in IVF is no higher than what occurs naturally. However, that is not true. No woman experiencing normal ovulation and conception spontaneously miscarries as many as six embryos, unless she is using fertility drugs.

The embryo transfer step in IVF evokes the most concern since it involves living human beings, not reproductive gametes (sperm and egg cells). Conception has already occurred at this point, and the embryo is on the way to manifesting his or her humanity. Some clinics transfer all the embryos. However, many IVF clinics engage in "quality control," selecting certain embryos for transfer and destroying others.[8] Essentially that is abortion.

The clinician knows that he will lose embryos. It is not a remote possibility but an expectation, proved by the fact that clinicians favor multiple transfers in order to maximize the possibility of at least one term pregnancy. It is difficult to support a technology that knowingly causes the death of several human beings.

If IVF is to be justified on moral grounds it must be conditioned on several key factors. First, the procedure should only involve married heterosexual couples.

Second, the ovum and sperm must be obtained from that couple, not from donors. Prenatal adoption, that is, the "adopting" of gametes left by couples who have had a baby and no longer need them, has gained popularity recently. That is another argument against ovarian hyperstimulation. We should not treat gametes like baseball trading cards.

Third, only one ovum should be fertilized and only one embryo transferred. If our goal is to replicate natural procreation, one should be sufficient. The loss of one human embryo is significant. We should avoid losing more than that.

IVF should not be used for experimental purposes. Preimplantation embryos should be accorded the same respect as newborn babies. They are unique human beings made in God's image, not laboratory rats.

Gamete Intrafallopian Transfer (GIFT)

GIFT differs from IVF only in that fertilization takes place inside the woman's body. Also unlike IVF, which involves the transfer of multiple embryos, GIFT involves the transfer of multiple ovum and sperm into the endometrial cavity, where conception, if it occurs, will take place.

GIFT, like IVF, has an overall success rate of 11 percent. The moral dilemma of selecting only "normal" embryos for transfer is eliminated here, yet the problem of harvesting multiple eggs remains, which means the potential for multiple embryo loss still exists. More important is the growing dependence on "selective termination," the aborting of selected "extra" embryos.

Uterine Lavage

In Chicago's Water Tower Place is a suite marked "Reproduction and Fertility Clinic," headed by Dr. Randolph Seed (no pun intended) and his veterinarian brother, Richard. They use a process called "artificial embryonation," which takes a human embryo from the uterus of a fertile

woman and places it in the womb of an infertile woman. Sur-
rogates are paid $250 to become pregnant with the husband's
sperm then have the pre-implantation embryo flushed out
and transferred to the uterus of the wife. The Seeds also offer
embryo adoption for couples in which both husband and
wife are unable to produce gametes.

Since 1983, several viable, term pregnancies have resulted from "flushing" pre-implantation embryos out of the uterus of a fertile woman and transferring the embryo to the
uterus of an infertile woman. Also known as Surrogate Embryo Transfer (SET), the procedure initially held promise for
women without ovaries or with premature ovarian failure. A
variation is the busy career woman who has her ovum inseminated by her husband's sperm and the embryo transferred to
the womb of a surrogate. Biologically the child belongs to the
married couple, but several legal issues remain unresolved,
much like the issues surrounding surrogate mothering in
general.

THIRD PARTY ARRANGEMENTS

Third-party birthing arrangements, such as surrogacy
and gamete or embryo donors, are fraught with hazard. Some
argue that such arrangements have biblical support, citing
the case of Abraham and Hagar (Genesis 16). They see that
situation as biblical justification for surrogate mothering and
AID. Ironically Hagar's surrogacy actually sustains some of
the arguments against surrogacy. It demonstrates what can
go wrong with that kind of arrangement.

Others justify surrogacy by citing the biblical provision
for Levirate marriage in Deuteronomy 25:5-6:

> When brothers live together and one of them dies and has no
> son, the wife of the deceased shall not be married outside the
> family to a strange man. Her husband's brother shall go in to
> her and take her to himself as wife and perform the duty of a
> husband's brother to her. And it shall be that the first-born
> whom she bears shall assume the name of his dead brother,
> that his name may not be blotted out from Israel.

Some say that that passage supports surrogacy. However, several features of the Levirate marriage differ significantly from surrogacy. One is the fact that in Levirate marriage the husband of the barren woman was dead, which is generally not the case with surrogate mothering.

Second, Levirate marriage was not permitted in every situation where a brother died. The death of a brother did not in itself entitle one to marry the widow and have children with her. The brothers were required to have lived together (v. 5), implying a business partnership. Today surrogacy usually involves strangers, which facilitates the very thing Levirate marriage was intended to prevent.

Third, Levirate marriage involved a marriage, not just a procreational relationship. The man and his sister-in-law became husband and wife. It was not a one-time relationship but God's means of providing for widows and orphans. It also provided a means for preserving the social and legal integrity of the family, as well as protecting the family's land and business holdings. Surrogate mothering and all other third-party birthing arrangements do not accomplish that.

The moral status of the pre-implantation embryo is often compromised by some forms of noncoital procreation. The medical community cannot be counted on to take a biblical stand regarding the personhood of unborn human beings. Most medical ethicists consider human embryos "potential persons," since they do not yet possess organ systems.

The charge against noncoital procreation deserves consideration. Exotic technology has altered our thinking about procreation, and bizarre definitions of "family" and "motherhood" have emerged as a result. Homosexual couples are now being considered families. The family will no doubt undergo further changes. When a South Dakota woman gave birth to twins conceived by her daughter and son-in-law, many struggled to sort out traditional notions of motherhood and family.

Courts are confused by our new technology as well. For example, a Tennessee judge was asked to decide the fate of seven cryo-preserved human embryos. After the last cycle of Junior and Mary Sue Davis's IVF treatment, seven embryos were left over, which the clinic kept for future use. Unexpectedly, the Davises divorced. Mr. Davis wanted the judge to treat the embryos as property, whereas Mrs. Davis considered them her children and asked the judge to award custody to her. That case and others that will follow require the wisdom of Solomon.

Much about the physiology and ethics of human procreation remains unknown. We do not know how IVF children will react to news of the circumstances surrounding their conception. What will the impact be on male-female relationships if further advances are made in noncoital procreation?

BIBLICAL CONCERNS

Procreation is seen by many as a fundamental tenet of humanness, the ultimate expression of one's personhood. From a biblical perspective the procreation of a human being brings into the world a unique and special individual made in the image and likeness of God (Genesis 1:26). The desire to procreate is a noble and natural aspiration. To seek to imitate God by "creating" life is not a selfish or self-indulgent goal.

In general the church has failed to recognize the special needs of childless couples, despite the fact that their numbers are increasing. Too often such couples only find understanding and empathy outside of the local church. Support groups are common outside the church but almost unheard of within the Christian community.

That is not to say that childless couples should be treated as we might the mentally disabled, with special classes or programs. But a listening ear, encouragement, and a genuine attempt to gain an appreciation for their needs and feelings should be offered freely. Childless couples, like single individuals, should find their greatest support and understanding within the Body of Christ. Those Christians capable of bearing children should demonstrate sensitivity and empathy for those who are unable to. In a day when churches sponsor softball teams, aerobics classes, and a variety of support groups, it does not seem out of line to consider sponsoring a support group for couples who want children but cannot have them.

THE RIGHT TO PROCREATE

In American culture, important issues often end up being referred to in the context of rights, and procreation is no exception. "Reproductive freedom" is a slogan feminists have successfully injected into society's vocabulary. Whereas they usually mean the right to be free from childbearing, those who desire children interpret it to mean they have the right to have children by whatever means available. If a woman has a fundamental right to prevent or terminate a pregnancy with the assistance of a physician, doesn't another woman also have the right to have a child with that same medical assistance?

It may be accurate to say that in America people have the constitutional right to bear children, just as they have the right to breathe clean air and drink clean water. However, no document can guarantee everyone perfect health.

From a biblical perspective human beings are to be subject to the lordship of Christ. Christians yield all their rights to His sovereignty. Although God commands us to "be fruitful and multiply" (Genesis 1:28), it is apparent that not everyone can fulfill that command, just as it is not possible for every person to fulfill the command to evangelize. Unmarried men and women do not have the right to procreate. Likewise, in our fallen state some bodies are incapable of bearing children. As with other abnormal physical conditions, infertility should receive medical attention. However, childlessness is not a medical condition and not amenable to medical treatment. Childlessness may be the result of a physical problem that may or may not be amenable to medical correction. Unfortunately, we have placed greater emphasis upon correcting the result than removing the cause.

Noncoital procreation technologies focus principally on childlessness. Couples spend enormous amounts of money, viewing such technologies as their last hope. We should carefully and prayerfully consider the consequences of looking to medicine for solutions to what are largely social problems.

CONCLUSION

Childlessness is certainly difficult, but it is not a life-threatening condition. The childless couple deserves our sympathy and understanding, just as we would empathize with anyone whose deepest ambitions and hopes are unfulfilled. Where infertility can be medically corrected a couple may want to pursue treatment.

Still, there are no guarantees in life. People throughout history have been forced to live with unfulfilled expectations. In the end, regardless of our circumstances, the Christian must determine whether he or she will accept God's grace as sufficient. Although the desire to have children is normal and admirable we must give serious thought to medical techniques that attempt to give man complete control over the entrance gates of life.

In a day when people find access to basic health care impossible due to rising costs, is it wise to allocate millions of dollars to medically assisted procreation, particularly when it is effective only 11 percent of the time?

QUESTIONS TO THINK ABOUT

1. Is there a biblical right to procreate? Explain.
2. What is the biblical definition of parenthood?
3. What arguments can be made for and against noncoital procreation?
4. Case Study: A Christian woman has been married twenty years. She is fertile, but her husband is sterile. They are considering artificial insemination by donor sperm. Is it right? Why or why not?

Part 3:

Issues in Life-Extension Medicine

6

SEVERELY HANDICAPPED NEWBORNS

B aby Girl Stanton is five weeks old. Born at twenty-eight weeks gestation, she weighed 800 grams. She had to be placed on a ventilator during her first day of life and since then has required high levels of oxygen. She suffered a pneumothorax (the buildup of air or gas in the area surrounding the lungs) at two weeks, but that was resolved with the insertion of a chest tube.

Then she suffered an episode that the staff thought was an intracranial bleed. Tests reveal that the hemorrhage was somewhere between a grade 2 and a grade 3 bleed. The baby was stabilized but still requires 55 percent oxygen to maintain adequate blood gases. The doctors fear infection. The infant has had cultures taken and is on antibiotics.

Her parents are in their early thirties. The father is an accountant, and the mother teaches biology at a local community college. They have been in daily attendance at the Neonatal Intensive Care Unit (NICU) and have spent a great deal of time talking with physicians and nursing staff as well as other NICU parents. They have witnessed several other crises in the busy twenty-bed NICU.

Now they are asking for more accurate information on their daughter's chances for normal existence. The neonatalogists explain that the difficulty in grading the extent of the bleed prevents their making an accurate prognosis. If the bleed is a grade 2, the infant has an approximately 83 percent chance of survival, with an 11 percent chance of major neurological handicap and a 39 percent chance of minor neurological handicap. If the bleed is a grade 3, survival chances are about the same, but the infant has a 35 percent chance of major neurological impairment and a 50 percent chance of minor impairment. The child will also likely experience bronchopulmonary dysplasia (a chronic lung disease).

Based on those prognostic indicators, the parents are requesting that aggressive life-prolonging treatments cease and that their child be allowed to die. The case has been referred to your ethics committee. What counsel would you offer?

A newborn lay in the nursery of a Bloomington, Indiana, hospital. The sign on his incubator and medical chart read "Do Not Feed," much like those at the zoo warning patrons not to feed the animals. It is incongruous not to feed a newborn, but those were the doctor's (and parents') orders. Under different circumstances the authorities would have been notified and the parents charged with neglect.[1]

In this case the special care nurses revolted, threatening to walk off the job if they weren't allowed to feed him. If they were refused, they demanded that he be moved off the floor. Linda McCabe, head nurse in the special care nursery, recalls seeing the child lying in his incubator with the sign taped overhead. "They had a lot of gall asking me to do that," she said. Maudeline Starbuck, chief nurse on the obstetrical floor, said, "It was very hard on my nurses. They felt like they were literally killing the baby." To quell the nurses' revolt, the hospital administration moved the child to a private room on the fourth floor and hired private nurses to watch and "comfort" him, but they were not allowed to give him anything.

As the hospital's lawyers and the parents wrangled over his fate in court, Baby Doe starved and dehydrated. As Lawrence Brodeur, the attorney representing Baby Doe, boarded a plane for Washington, D.C., to file an emergency appeal with Supreme Court Justice Thurgood Marshall, the child began to hemorrhage. Blood oozed from his nose and mouth, but the Indiana Supreme Court had already upheld the "right" of the parents to withhold "artificial life support" from their child. Three times Baby Doe stopped breathing, only to fight his way back to life.

At one point Dr. Owens, the child's physician, and another hospital staff physician, Dr. Schaffer, engaged in a heated argument over who was in charge of the child. Owens asserted his authority to order "nontreatment." Schaffer insisted that he was acting in the best interests of the child and intended to take him to the special care nursery and feed him. Imagine two physicians arguing openly over whether to save or take human life!

Justice Thurgood Marshall sent word to the child's attorney that he could not be disturbed and that the child would still be alive in the morning, at which time he would hear the appeal. Two hours later Baby Doe died—the victim of parental, medical, and judicial neglect. The cause of death? Chemical pneumonia, due to the regurgitation and aspiration of his own stomach acid.

Baby Doe's mistake was to be born with Down syndrome. A blocked esophagus rendered him unable to swallow, a condition easily corrected by surgery. But because of the untreatable nature of Down syndrome, his parents decided not to treat him at all. They chose death for their son.

Tragically, several couples were denied the opportunity to adopt Baby Doe. Those families included couples who already had Down syndrome children. Many such children lead happy, productive lives.

NEONATAL MEDICINE: MIRACLE OR MENACE?

Is there such a thing as a life so burdensome that death is better? Are some lives "not worthy of being lived"? Such questions are regularly asked by those who care for imperiled newborns. Though neonatal intensive care units and special care nurseries have saved many lives, a growing number of medical professionals question whether they should do that as often and aggressively as they do. They ask whether we should continue to use the technology currently implemented to save imperiled newborns when such babies often require a lifetime of special medical care. Can a society with limited health care resources be committed to saving every baby, regardless of the kind of life the child will lead?

Is it a "miracle" to save a severely handicapped child from death only to give him a life of surgeries, dependence on others, and being tethered to machines? Is it fair to save that life when it places enormous financial and emotional hardships on the family? Aggressive treatment of an imperiled newborn may succeed in saving her life but at what economic, social, and emotional cost? Those are questions both parents and care givers are asking.

Neonatalogists and pediatricians face serious dilemmas. Unlike older patients, who have a medical history and are usually able to communicate for themselves, newborns represent a "clean slate." There is no backdrop to which progress or regress can be compared. The infant cannot tell us where she hurts. Prognosis is difficult since basic motor skills, mental capacity, and so on will not appear for months, if at all. Consequently, care givers often face the difficulty of determining the long-term outcome of certain treatments. A physician may have no way of knowing whether his or her tiny patient will be a miracle survivor or a medical "burden."

A number of studies have been conducted to determine the "quality of life" enjoyed by neonatal survivors. A study conducted at the Milton S. Hershey Medical Center in Pennsylvania researched a group of children born between 1973 and 1976 who had been born with serious impairments. The study followed them until they were forty months old. Thirty-five percent were handicapped, 17 percent severely. The severe handicaps included major visual impairment, hydrocephalus, and spastic quadriplegia, a form of cerebral palsy in which all four limbs are spastic. The study also revealed that those children who had been ventilated at birth (placed on a respirator) had a 72 percent handicap rate, whereas those who had not been ventilated had a 19 percent handicap rate.[2]

At first glance, those numbers suggest that aggressive medical treatment of handicapped newborns is detrimental. In general, newborns less than 1000 grams birth-weight who survive after aggressive neonatal care do have an increased likelihood of lifelong impairments or handicap. However, many children survive with few or no impairments—children who would not have lived without aggressive care. Other studies have yielded similar results.

Children born at less than 650 grams generally have a 20 percent survival rate, with a 90 percent chance of lifelong disability. That means that 90 percent of those families will face continual medical treatment, surgeries, and so on, if the child survives. However, there is a 10 percent chance that he will survive with no serious lifelong disability.

Physicians attempt to inform parents of the facts of their baby's condition and to present whatever relevant medical options are available; yet parents' beliefs or biases may permit a broader or narrower range of options than are considered "standard medical judgment." The child's parents may opt to proceed with aggressive care, citing a belief that human life is sacred. Or, as in the case of Baby Doe, where his medical condition required not neonatal ICU but a fairly routine surgical procedure, his parents may choose to allow him to die. In both situations physicians played the role not only of medical technologists but of ethicists.

EUGENICS AT THE ENTRANCE GATES OF LIFE

Many decisions regarding the fate of handicapped babies are made before the children are born. Genetic screening techniques such as Alpha-Fetoprotein screening (AFP) or chorion villus sampling (CVS) are used to detect congenital defects prenatally. Those prenatal tests are so institutionalized in modern obstetrical practice that courts have awarded monetary damages to couples whose physician did not advise them that such tests were available.

Consequently, many obstetricians practice defensive medicine, advising patients about the availability of tests and abortion should a defect be found. That makes it difficult for a pro-life physician unwilling to conduct "search and destroy" missions. In a study of women's attitudes regarding aborting "defective" preborn children, only 71 out of 300 said they would not abort a child even if there was conclusive evidence that it would be born handicapped.[3] Clearly a sizable majority would abort a handicapped child.

Aborting a child because it has a birth defect is pure eugenics—the belief that the quality of the human race can be improved by controlling human procreation and by excluding those who do not meet certain criteria. The philosophy was adopted by Nazi doctors and has even been practiced in Romania. To exclude babies that do not fit a particular design, despite whether humanitarian verbiage is used to justify it, is no different from Hitler's exterminative medicine program against the Jews and other "undesirables."

The basic right to life is crowded out by other considerations. Infanticide is made to look humane. More than a few within the medical community are willing to let babies die when they are unwilling or uncertain that they can heal them. A growing number of physicians believe we should not flex the muscles of our medical technology to pump life into a newborn who will never understand the significance of what we have done, the meaninglessness of his existence, or the burden he brings upon his family. I find it difficult to maintain a high respect for human life when in reality it is only human life at the prescribed level that is respected. What value is there in holding a conditionally high view of human life? Only when life is of a humanly defined "high quality" is it valued in today's society.

I do not pretend to know why God allows severely handicapped newborns to be born. I do not know why God gives couples children who will never be able to call them "Mommy" or "Daddy," who will never be able to run or throw a ball or climb into a school bus. However, I know it is not right to kill those children.

A survey of pediatricians in Massachusetts revealed that 54 percent do not recommend surgery for infants like Baby Doe. Sixty-six percent would not recommend surgery for infants born with spina bifida.[4] One survey of Bay Area pediatricians found that 22 percent would recommend nontreatment for infants with Down syndrome but no other complications and more than 50 percent would recommend nontreatment in cases where other complications were present.[5] Only 1 percent of pediatricians and 3 percent of surgeons indicated that they could not accept a nontreatment decision in those situations.

Some would not only accept a nontreatment decision but would, if immune from criminal prosecution, actively intervene to end a handicapped child's life. Raymond Duff states, "Once the decision for non-treatment has been made, the means taken do not really matter. Euthanasia, either passive or active, can be a safe and humane choice in dealing with selective tragedies."[6] How can euthanasia be "safe" for any infant? In other words, once death has been chosen for an infant, the means of death is irrelevant. Duff is not alone in advocating physician-administered death for imperiled newborns. Michael Tooley, professor of philosophy at the University of Western Australia, argues that in order to have a right to something one must be capable of desiring that thing.[7] He contends that the defective newborn does not have a right to life because it is incapable of wanting that.

Clearly Tooley has little regard for handicapped newborns. If he is consistent in his logic, then he does not respect other handicapped individuals, particularly those with mental disabilities, either. In reality, many disabled people exhibit a greater desire to live than some who are considered healthy. Like all subjective criteria, Tooley's desire-oriented standard is pathetically arbitrary. How much desire is sufficient to guarantee a right to life? In Tooley's mind, the right to life is not a right at all but a preference, which others are free to supersede.

The denial of personhood is at the root of infanticide. Deeming imperiled newborns nonpersons pits the weak against the powerful, the voiceless against those who have voice. Quality of life decisions, whether made by physicians or parents, fail to take into account the moral integrity of the medical profession. What happens to the medical professional who assumes the role of executioner when he fails in his role as healer? What happens to the doctor-patient relationship when the physician abandons the principle of "first do no harm"?

Of course, physicians can claim that they are only complying with the wishes of the family, but they cannot escape the fact that families make decisions largely based upon the medical information received from the physician. Rarely do couples make a decision that contradicts the advice of their doctor. The average couple is unprepared for the emotions and the blur of activity that characterize the typical neonatal intensive care unit, not to mention the bombardment of medical terminology and intensity of the therapies under consideration. How can they keep up with the mass of information?

Perhaps most physicians would have serious ethical problems with a colleague who did not give full disclosure to the parents of an imperiled newborn, yet more than a few doctors believe that parents are incapable of taking an active role in treatment decisions, since much of the information is technical. Sometimes the physician has firm opinions about an acceptable quality of life, and those opinions affect the quality of medical care he offers to particular babies. His bias means that certain treatment options are left off the "menu." Since most parents have no experience with the complexities of neonatal care, it is relatively easy for a physician to guide them to the decision he deems best, rather than allowing them to decide for themselves after hearing the full range of options.

Parents would be well advised to quiz their doctors on their attitude toward the sanctity of human life well before the issue arises. I am not suggesting that parents provoke an adversarial relationship with their physicians. But communication between parents and physicians could facilitate better care and make decision making easier, should difficulties arise.

Some neonatal units operate under a standard some call the "wait until near certainty" approach. This approach assumes that every newborn is viable and should receive treatment until it is certain or near certain that he will die. When that point is reached parents may opt for nontreatment or the termination of treatment. Generally, most Christians would support this approach, provided that data regarding the child's condition is conclusive, that is, that continued treatment would certainly be futile.

Even here, the term *futile* should not be taken to mean that continued treatment would be futile in restoring a quality of life preferable to the parents and medical personnel; instead, it must mean continued treatment would not be medically beneficial. And "medically beneficial" means that the proposed treatment or therapy provides its intended benefit, that is, reduction or elimination of pain, restoration of function, or improvement in the overall health of the patient. If an antibiotic will eliminate an infection or virus, then it can be considered to be medically beneficial, even though the patient's overall health may not be good. If the medical treatment being considered can be expected to be medically beneficial then it should be used. However, if the best medical judgment is that such treatment would not be beneficial and the child is going to die regardless, then the treatment may be withheld or withdrawn.

THE ROLE OF ECONOMICS AND FAMILY STABILITY

Richard Lamm, the former governor of Colorado, caused a stir during his term by stating that he did not approve of giving intensive medical treatment and therapy to babies who could only roll over after a full year of treatment. He believed that the money budgeted for such children would be better spent on those with a higher quality of life. (Lamm also suggested that the elderly who are chronically ill and require ongoing, expensive medical care should accept their "duty to die" and get out of the way.)

There is a growing movement to ration health care in the U.S., including proposals to limit medical care for seriously ill newborns. Peter Singer, a bioethicist from Australia, suggests that some newborns be killed at birth because they do not meet his criteria of "personhood." Francis Crick, the Nobel laureate for his codiscovery of DNA, suggests that we not declare a newborn a "person" until three days after birth, following a battery of tests. (He also wants society to adopt a mandatory death law for people past the age of eighty.)

The bottom line to those proposals is money. The rising cost of health care is undeniable, and it can be extremely expensive to care for imperiled newborns and to sustain their lives once they leave the NICU. Who pays for that care? Is it moral for anyone to receive medical care for which he or she cannot pay? This subject will be addressed more fully in chapter 12.

Whether or not we want economics to play a role in medical decisions concerning imperiled newborns, it does. Financial resources for most people are finite. Who pays when a family is unable?

The question of family stability comes into play as well. Divorce is not uncommon among parents of imperiled newborns who do survive. Siblings sometimes resent the amount of time, attention, and financial resources allocated to care for a handicapped brother or sister. Everyone in the family has to make sacrifices.

Where does such a family find relief? Respite centers provide some help, as do community mental health agencies. However, in the long run, the care of a handicapped individual can create tremendous strain on family members. Should that be a factor in making treatment decisions concerning imperiled newborns?

Finances are a tangible, measurable commodity. Love, compassion, and commitment are not. Whereas the family finances can be spelled out, no one can predict how each member of the family will accept deprivation and sacrifice for the sake of one needy member.

Thus the spiritual resources of a family are crucial. A family-values inventory should be taken to establish what is really important. For example, the family should consider how important it is to have a nice house, yearly vacations, private education, eight hours of sleep per night, and so on. They may need to consider as well the role of hardship in building character. Couples should consider what impact a special needs child may have on their marriage and what qualities each of them can offer to strengthen the marriage and family relationships. Medical decisions ought not to be based solely on such an inventory, but it can be helpful in determining a family's strengths and weaknesses so that others can be enlisted to help. A child with special needs can bring out the best, or worst, in a family.

CONCLUSIONS

Medical decision making concerning imperiled newborns is a process. There is rarely only one decision at stake. Each day presents new dilemmas and possibilities. Uncertainty is a frequent visitor to the NICU. Every baby and every family is different. Yet one thing remains constant—the need to respect and protect human life when it is most vulnerable.

The question we ought to ask is, "Are we willing to accept the babies God gives us?" not, "Should all babies be allowed to live?" The moral integrity of the medical community should be such that we can trust them not to kill when unable to heal. Yet living in a fallen world means we have no guarantees.

QUESTIONS TO THINK ABOUT

1. What factors should be considered in deciding on the treatment of severely imperiled newborns?
2. How much of a role should economics and family stability play in medical decisions concerning imperiled newborns?
3. Is there such a thing as a life unworthy to be lived?
4. Can allowing a baby to die be regarded as beneficial?
5. How can a local church help families with handicapped members?

7

ORGAN TRANSPLANTS

The question of harvesting and transplanting human organs and tissues is a complex one. Some of the questions surrounding the procurement and use of human body parts are:

- Are bodily organs, tissues, and fluids "property" to be disposed of by whatever means one chooses, including donation or sale?

- Who owns the bodies of the deceased? Do property rights extend to genetic identity, to individuals, or to the species? Does the state own human bodies, as it owns wildlife?

- Who should make decisions affecting the acquisition of tissues, cells, and organs, and under what circumstances should such acquisition be permitted or denied?

- Should technologies, inventions, or treatments that incorporate the use of human cells and tissues be patentable?

- Is organ harvesting and transplantation a violation of the sovereignty of God?

- Should those who have abused their bodies with drugs, alcohol, or cigarettes be recipients of organ transplants?

- Is organ harvesting and transplantation a form of cannibalism?

The practice of solid organ substitution has become a billion-dollar-per-year business in the U.S., particularly since the discovery of powerful immunosuppressant drugs, such as cyclosporine, which help to prevent organ rejection. The prominent question today is not whether we can successfully transplant human organs, but whether we will find enough organs to meet the growing demand.

There is no question that transplanting organs is effective. For example, kidney transplants from cadavers succeed in extending the lives of more than 85 percent of those who receive them. Lives are being saved by harvesting and transplanting the organs of dead people. As many as seven people can benefit from one donor.

The death rate among those waiting for a major organ is quite high, however. Organ procurement organizations indicate that some 15,000 people die each year while waiting for suitable organs. The media plays a significant role in portraying the plight of some, especially children. National television has aired direct pleas from parents for organ donations to save the lives of their children.

THE DECREASE IN AVAILABLE TRANSPLANT ORGANS

Aside from an increase in demand, several important factors affect the dearth of available organs, for example, more stringent regulations concerning seatbelts, helmets for motorcyclists, handguns, drunk driving, and the drinking age. Fewer traumatic deaths mean fewer donors.

Another reason organ procurement lags behind demand is the ambivalence many people feel about death and dying. Many praise organ donation, with some polls showing that as many as 70 percent of the general population support it in principle, but only 16 percent carry a donor card or have indicated a willingness to donate their own organs.

Currently a federal law, the Required Request Act, requires medical personnel to ask families of dying patients to consider donating their loved one's organs. Ironically, as more families are asked to donate, fewer are giving consent. Why do so many say no?

Common reasons for denying a request for organ donation are: (1) the fear that the person is really not dead; (2) the view that organ procurement is mutilation of the body; (3) fear about life after death or that removing major organs may prevent resurrection. The same reasons are also given by many people who refuse to sign donor cards.

ARGUMENTS IN FAVOR OF
ORGAN DONATION AND TRANSPLANT

1. Organ transplants save lives.

Roughly 70,000 people need a major organ transplant. Doesn't saving lives justify using organs that would otherwise decay? If we really believe in the sanctity of human life, we should use our skills to enable people to live longer and healthier lives. Organ transplants have proved to be an effective means to that end.

2. Organ transplants are cost effective.

A kidney transplant costs approximately $125,000. Kidney dialysis costs approximately $30,000 per year, so a lifetime of treatment could cost several hundred thousand dollars. Even when the cost of continued care after transplant is factored in— cyclosporine (anti-rejection drugs), additional surgery, and so on—the cost of the transplant remains less than kidney dialysis.

3. Organ donation and transplant is an illustration of the biblical principle of self-sacrifice.

Jesus said, "Greater love has no one than this, that one lay down his life for his friends" (John 15:13). He taught that it is honorable for a person to be willing to sacrifice for his friends, even if it means giving up his own life.

We have national holidays to honor those who gave their lives for freedom. We make heroes of those who risk their own well-being for the sake of others. Donating organs is also a heroic act.

4. Donating organs is good stewardship.

Christians are encouraged to practice good stewardship in every area of life. We encourage planned giving whereby believers leave some of their estate to particular ministries following their death. Shouldn't we be urged to make a gift of our organs also? Donating one's organs is an extension of the recycling habit.

5. Scripture teaches that we are to do good to all men, especially those who are believers (Galatians 6:10).

It is a Christian's obligation to help people when it is within his or her power to do so. Paul teaches that we do not live nor die for ourselves (Romans 14:7). As the Lord Jesus demonstrated with His own death on the cross, we live for others. So within the context of a Christian theory of obligation, can we make an argument for allowing someone else to live by donating organs that we no longer need?

The above arguments hinge on one's concept of the human body. If the body is viewed as incidental to personhood, then one may be permitted to donate or even sell human organs. However, if the body is viewed as essential to personhood, then selling human body parts may be immoral.

ORGAN PROCUREMENT

In November 1991, a man entered the Oak Park, Michigan, Post Office and gunned down several employees before turning the weapon on himself. Later that day he was said to be "brain dead." The next day he was pronounced dead and his organs were immediately removed for transplant. Did that donation negate the harm done to his victims and their families?

Some argue that death row inmates should be required to donate their organs. If organ donation is in itself beneficial, then perhaps it should be obligatory, a moral imperative like rescuing a drowning person or preventing a blind person from walking out into traffic.

If there is a moral duty to donate, is there a moral way to distribute organs? Indeed, if bequeathing one's organs for transplant is a moral duty, we'd better stop calling it a "donation." *Procurement* would be a more accurate term.

Today donating organs is viewed as strictly voluntary. We are free not to donate if we so choose.

However, a growing number of proponents advocate changing the emphasis from donation to obligation, which would focus public policy on the issue of rejection, not informed consent. That is, if we have a moral duty to donate, then public policy should eliminate the option to reject "requests" to donate.

In reality, the donor is seldom given the option of refusal simply because he is unconscious, near death, or already dead. Usually the family is approached for consent to the donation. Family refusal is still a significant problem, with denials as high as 70 percent.

TYPES OF DONATION

Express Donation

In an express donation, the donor leaves written instructions that she wishes to donate her organs. Such instructions may be found on the back of a driver's license, a donor card, or in the person's advance directive for health care.

Sales

Some defend selling organs as a way to respect an individual's autonomy while increasing the supply of organs. At present, no state permits the sale of human organs, and the National Organ Transplant Act and the Uniform Anatomical Gift Act forbid it. Most states made organ sales illegal in the mid-eighties.

Payment to blood donors was common in the U.S. not long ago, and donors of semen still receive payment. If we can purchase blood from people, why not a kidney? Nearly one-third of all kidney transplants last year involved kidneys from living donors.

Objections to the sale of organs rest primarily on concerns about exploitation, particularly of the poor. If poverty motivates a person to sell a kidney it could be seen as a redistribution of health from the poor to the rich, which would likely become exploitative and unjust.

A second objection to the sale of organs is the idea that human tissue—particularly organs that are irreplaceable and non-renewable—would come to be treated like pork bellies, a mere commercial commodity. In a worst case scenario, one day human organs could be traded on the Chicago Board of Trade.

An alternative to the sale of organs is the offer of a $1,000 death benefit to families who agree to donate their loved one's organs, with the funds applied to medical or funeral costs. That proposal avoids the perception of commerce in human body parts since any organ is worth far more than $1,000, but it would be a gesture of appreciation toward survivors.

Expropriation

Just as the state often expropriates land it needs for roads or other state use, it could conceivably take possession of human bodies upon declaration of death and remove desired tissues, then release the body to the family for burial. However, few support that approach since it is not politically feasible or ethically acceptable.

Abandonment

One suggestion is to use organs from people who have been abandoned or have no surviving family members. Although this approach has wide appeal, it differs little from expropriation. Although the state takes control of abandoned assets, it does not seem ethically appropriate for the state to assume ownership of human bodies.

Presumed Consent

Generally, presumed consent means that in the absence of written evidence to the contrary we can assume that the deceased would have been willing to donate his or her organs. Belgium, Sweden, and other European countries use presumed consent as a way of increasing their supply of organs.

Several objections can be raised to presumed consent. First, it is possible to presume incorrectly. Advocates contend that a computerized registry of people who decline to make donations could be accessible to all organ procurement organizations and hospitals. Unfortunately, we cannot always trust the accuracy of computers. If they cannot keep accurate credit histories, how could they keep tabs on our views of organ donation? A mistake on my credit history is fairly easy to correct. What means of correction will compensate for an error in organ donation?

Presumed consent undermines the basic principles of privacy and autonomy, particularly due process. Although it can be argued that a dead person no longer has the right of privacy and due process, the fact is that he does. Grave robbing is still a crime. Furthermore, presumed consent presupposes that the absence of objection constitutes consent. If I fail to answer a knock at my door, it does not mean the caller has permission to enter. The same principle applies to organ donation. In sum, organs should not be removed unless expressed, informed consent is obtained.

MORAL CONCERNS ABOUT ORGAN TRANSPLANTS

1. Harvesting and transplanting body parts may cause people to look at the human body as just a collection of parts.

Organ transplants, although they evoke humanitarian feelings, are seen by some as treating the human body like a junked car whose parts are appropriated to keep another car running. Rather than regarding the human body as an integrated aspect of personhood, the body is viewed as incidental to personhood.

2. Scripture teaches that we do not own our bodies; they belong to God (1 Corinthians 6:19).

Do we have the right to give away that which does not belong to us? Is it possible for organ recipients to glorify God with their bodies while suppressing the immune system with drugs in order to keep their bodies from rejecting an organ? But those who have received organs are quick to respond that the risk of cancer, tumors, and other complications associated with the transplant is worth a longer life.

3. Organ transplants may usurp God's sovereignty.

One could assert that God gave each set of organs to each individual, not to the general human race. A person's body, internally and externally, makes up his or her "being." It is nontransferable.

In addition, it could be argued that God sovereignly establishes the length of our lives. Are organ transplants an attempt to interfere with His plan? Actually that argument could be made concerning every medical intervention. Wouldn't removing a ruptured appendix violate God's sovereignty as surely as transplanting an organ?

The only way that argument can stand on its own is if we adopt the belief that God's providential care for His creation means He personally and directly acts in every situation concerning our lives, rather than permitting "secondary" events (influences such as medicine) to accomplish His purpose.

Likewise, the argument presupposes that God's sovereignty is predeterministic, that every event that happens to a person is either directly caused by God or directly prevented by God. Yet that requires a belief that humans are robots.

4. An association has been made between organ transplants and brain death.

Of all the concerns about organ transplants, the fear that organs may be taken before the donor is really dead is the most troubling. Though no one openly admits it, our current definitions, at least in part, facilitate organ "procurement." If there were no use for human tissues or organs, the need for criteria to make an early determination of death would be less critical.

A perusal of the relevant literature suggests that the change in the definition of death was at least partially due to the prevalence of organ transplants. Considerable debate continues to divide the medical community on the issue of brain death. If medical experts are split on this matter, is it any wonder that individuals and families remain uncomfortable with it?

In many states, the guiding principle for determining death is the Uniform Determination of Death Act (UDDA), which states: "An individual who has sustained either (i) irreversible cessation of circulatory and respiratory functions, or (ii) irreversible cessation of all functions of the entire brain, including the brain stem, is dead. A determination of death must be made in accordance with accepted medical standards."

On the surface, that appears to be a straightforward definition. However, it is not as simple as it seems. The UDDA refers to the functions of respiration, circulation, and the brain. But in some instances resuscitative measures can restore respiratory or circulatory functions. People can survive heart attacks and strokes today because of the ability to restore those functions.

How many times have we heard news stories about people who were declared "brain dead" or "clinically dead" but were being "kept alive by artificial means"? That suggests that it is possible to be both dead and alive, which is physiologic fiction. You are either alive or dead, not both.

The loss of organ function does not necessarily mean the organs have been destroyed. Irreversible loss of organ function is deduced from other evidence and is not alone an empirical, observable conclusion. Who can look at an unconscious body and determine that the lungs will never function again? Not until we biopsy the lungs to discover structural change—decay, perhaps—could we conclude that irreversible loss of respiratory function has occurred.

To ascertain death we ideally should look for organ destruction, not the loss of organ function. However, that approach to determining death renders organs unsuitable for transplant.

Many clinical signs of brain death can be mimicked. Fixed pupils and the absence of motor activities do not automatically indicate irreversible damage to the brain stem. "Flat" (isoelectric) electroencepholagrams (EEG) have been recorded in survivors of hypothermia, cerebral anoxia, and herpes simplex encephalitis.

5. Organ harvesting and transplanting tend to diminish the awesomeness of the "donor's" demise.

The frequency and efficacy of transplanting organs diminishes the awesomeness of the donor's demise. Family members of hopeful organ recipients have been known to request prayer that a donor would be found, seemingly oblivious to the fact that a person must die in order to become a donor. Although we cannot fault a family for their concern, can it ever be said to be within God's will to pray that one person would benefit by the physical death of another?

At some point the value of a patient seems to be derived from his or her potential as an organ donor. In that respect organ procurement and transplant is a sophisticated form of cannibalism.

ARTIFICIAL ORGANS

Barney Clark was the first human to receive an artificial heart transplant. Going into surgery, he knew as well as his doctors that his life would not be extended appreciably. His operation sparked a debate not only on the wisdom of using human beings as medical guinea pigs but on the wisdom of using artificial organs. Currently, the artificial heart is used as a "bridge" during open heart surgery, or until a donor heart can be obtained.

Research continues to develop artificial organs, limbs, skin, and so on. Grafting synthetic human skin is a common treatment for burn patients. Artificial limbs provide mobility and dexterity to amputees. Generally speaking, an artificial limb or organ transplant does not present the moral complexities of a cadaver organ substitution since there is no "donor," and obtaining the organ or limb did not involve someone else's death.

However, the search for human life extension through the use of donor or artificial organs seems to involve more than a simple desire to help dying people live longer. Is that desire motivated by humanitarian, altruistic motives, or is it another manifestation of man's desire to control his own destiny and to strive for immortality? At least in part the motivation appears to come from the humanistic belief that man is potentially perfectible, albeit in a physical sense.

XENOGRAFTING

The debate on the use of animal organs for transplant into humans (xenograft) was fueled when the Loma Linda Medical Center in California tried to transplant the heart of a baboon into a little girl several years ago. The child died shortly after the experiment when her body rejected the animal tissue.

Since then researchers have focused on developing immunosuppressant drugs to keep the human body from rejecting animal tissue. But progress has been slow. Proponents of the research argue that, if successful, thousands of lives will be saved worldwide.

However, such a practice, if medically possible, would raise additional moral and legal questions that society presently is not capable of answering. In particular, does it violate biblical principles of morality related to the differentiation between humans and animals?

WHO GETS SCARCE ORGANS?

A central issue concerning organ transplants is who should receive scarce organs. If an organ procurement organization has six people on its waiting list with near identical tissue matches when a heart becomes available, who should receive it? Should it go to the person who has been on the list the longest or to the person with the worst health? What if either person is a chain smoker, overweight, a heavy drinker, or negligent in taking high blood pressure medicine? Do such people even belong on waiting lists for organs?

Should a convicted murderer receive a kidney transplant when a responsible, law-abiding father of four needs the same kidney? Should age determine who receives a transplant? Should the president of the United States receive better treatment than an auto mechanic? Should one's ability to pay continue to be a factor, giving the rich priority over the poor?

THE USE OF ORGANS FROM IMPERILED NEWBORNS

The Loma Linda Medical Center again sparked international debate in 1987 when it announced that it would begin using organs from anencephalic newborns (babies born without part or all of their brain).

Since many such babies do not meet the brain death criteria established in the Uniform Determination of Death Act (UDDA), which requires the irreversible cessation of all functions of the brain, critics of the Loma Linda Center's decision argued that it constituted removing organs from living donors. Critics also argue that the policy ignores the fact that there is no clear consensus on a definition of death. In view of the fact that ambiguities still remain, there is considerable anxiety among the general population regarding physicians who remove organs before a person is truly dead.

An additional objection to using organs of anencephalics is the fact that the potential for increasing the supply of organs for pediatric transplant is overestimated. Fewer than ten patients each year would benefit from this kind of transplant, since most anencephalic newborns are not suitable donors and many do not survive long after birth.

In March 1992, an anencephalic girl, "Baby Theresa," was delivered in a Fort Lauderdale, Florida, hospital by cesarean section at the request of her parents. She was treated aggressively, including placement on a ventilator and was given other medical treatments not normally given to anencephalic newborns. Why? Because her parents wanted to donate her organs to other children.

However, Baby Theresa's neonatologist, Brian Udell, refused to remove Theresa's organs until she met the legal criteria for death, which meant that her brain stem had to cease functioning. A nationwide debate ensued when the parents found an attorney who argued before Broward County Circuit Judge Estella Moriarty that the legal criteria for brain death was meant for people who at one time had had a whole, intact brain, which Baby Theresa had never had. Therefore, the court could issue an order allowing the removal of Baby Theresa's organs because she did not have a brain.

Although we may sympathize with Baby Theresa's parents and can understand their desire to bring good from their tragic loss, we are purchasing problems on a credit plan if physicians begin to take organs from people who are not dead. In Baby Theresa's case, death would be determined not on strictly medical criteria but on a philosophical analysis, that is, the death of the higher brain constitutes the death of the person.

The most compelling argument against using organs from anencephalic infants is the fact that it would require a change in the Uniform Anatomical Gift Act. Presently the act does not allow hearts, kidneys, and livers to be removed from "donors" who are still alive. The criteria concerning brain death could be changed also so that those who have lost the functions of the higher brain can be classified as dead, thus becoming organ "donors." However, changing either the Act or criteria regarding brain death to mean death of the higher brain would make the determination of death a philosophical matter, not a medical one.

The problem is that anencephalic children are not dead; they are dying. Few survive more than a few days. Yet despite that desperate condition, they do not meet the UDDA criteria for a determination of death. Those criteria are designed to be met by strict empirical means. Declaring a person dead while his heart, lungs, and kidneys continue to function is not a scientific judgment but a philosophical one—indeed a dangerous one. Therefore, to remove organs from an anencephalic infant means killing one child in order to save another.

That is a terribly flawed approach to ethics. When it becomes lawful to kill a person because his death will benefit another or because he will die soon anyway, that justification may be used in other situations. It may be applied to unconscious, incompetent patients who are terminally ill, or to other newborns with organ failure. The "logic" could also be applied to other irreversibly brain damaged persons whose "higher brain" has been lost. Advocates of changing the UDDA assert that safeguards could be implemented to insure that we do not travel down that "slippery slope," but once the Act is changed, it will be easier to relax standards further. Legislative solutions are fraught with hazard. It is relatively easy to amend legislation once public and media scrutiny have been diverted to other issues.

Another reason for rejecting the proposal to declare anencephalics dead in order to increase organ supply is the fact that in doing so it is possible inadvertently to decrease the number of organs available for adult transplants. Consider this. Currently more families are being asked to donate their loved ones' organs than ever before, due to the enactment of

Required Request legislation. However, fewer people are consenting to donation. Why?

One reason is that people fear that organs will be removed before a loved one is really dead. The average American is confused by existing definitions of "brain death." How can that confusion be eliminated or alleviated if we alter the criteria to make brain death even more ambiguous? Furthermore, is the proposal certain to result in increased donations when existing criteria that require whole brain death have not?

CONCLUSIONS

Organ transplants, like few other medical procedures, push the limits of traditional understanding of the value of an individual life. At first glance the subject seems to lack grounds for controversy as the intent of an organ transplant is to help a dying person live. However, we must concern ourselves not only with the ends but with the means employed to achieve them.

QUESTIONS TO THINK ABOUT

1. Who owns human body parts? Are human bodies like other personal property, which we are free to dispose of as we desire?
2. Are organ transplants a valid means of extending human life?
3. Assuming organ transplants are morally acceptable, what is ethical/unethical about the sale of organs?
4. Do organ transplants violate the sovereignty of God?
5. Should an alcoholic and a nondrinker be equally eligible for liver transplants?

8

GENETIC ENGINEERING

If any one age really attains, by eugenics and scientific education, the power to make its descendants what it pleases, all
men who live after it are patients of that power. They are
weaker, not stronger: for though we have put wonderful machines in their hands we have pre-ordained how they are to
use them. . . . The real picture is that of one dominant age . . .
which resists all previous ages most successfully and domi-
nates all subsequent ages most irresistibly, and thus is the
real master of the human species. But even within this master
generation (itself an infinitesimal minority of the species) the
power will be exercised by a minority smaller still. Man's con-
quest of Nature, if the dreams of the scientific planners are
realized, means the rule of a few hundreds of men over billions upon billions of men. There neither is nor can there be
any simple increase in power on Man's side. Each new power
won by man is a power over man as well. Each advance
leaves him weaker as well as stronger. In every victory be-
sides being the general who triumphs, man is also the prisoner who follows the triumphal carriage.

C. S. Lewis, *The Abolition of Man*

The field of genetics has undergone an explosion since the
days of Mendel. The study of genetics once focused on
crossbreeding and other benign types of research. Hybrid-
ization was the peak of sophistication until the development

of techniques such as gene splicing using recombinant DNA technologies. Recombinant DNA involves the splicing of DNA strands from different organisms and inserting the resulting combination into a host virus or bacterium where it reproduces itself. The technique has been used successfully in agriculture and in the production of certain drugs.

Society has already reaped the benefits of genetic research. Not only have applications of recombinant DNA technology raised larger livestock and quick-growing corn, but we have also produced synthetic drugs that benefit those who are allergic to other medicines. Without doubt, current research has positive benefits. Yet like the moon, genetic research has a dark side.

GENETIC SCREENING

In the past, genetic counseling for a pregnant woman meant an evaluation of her family's history and a physical examination to determine the potential for genetic disorders. Research produced statistical information concerning the risk of birth defects.

With the discovery of DNA analysis, the practice of screening pregnant women to determine the presence of genetic defects in unborn children has become almost standard obstetrical care. "Wrongful birth" relates to judgments against doctors for medical negligence. They neglected to advise pregnant patients of the possibility for genetic screening for defects and the availability of abortion if a defect was found. Consequently, when children are born with a variety of birth defects, parents are prompted to sue for wrongful birth on grounds that they would have aborted the child had they been properly informed. In fact, the legal climate emanating from wrongful birth lawsuits has changed the doctor-patient relationship to such an extent that many physicians no longer deliver babies or, if they do, they practice defensive medicine by ordering prenatal screening and advising their patients that abortion is available to "treat" a defective child.

Alpha-fetoprotein, Amniocentesis

One of the most common genetic tests used today is alpha-fetoprotein (AFP), a procedure made possible by the successful tissue culture and cytogenetic study of amniotic fluid cells. Originally developed to detect Rh factor incompatibility prenatally, the test is performed by amniocentesis around fifteen to twenty weeks gestation by the removal of amniotic fluid from the amniotic sac, the bag of water in which the unborn child "swims" as he or she develops. AFP is used primarily to detect single gene defects such as Down syndrome, neural tube defects such as spina bifida, and ventral wall defects in the heart.

AFP is usually recommended to women beyond age thirty-five. It is also recommended for women who have had children with congenital defects, have a family history of congenital defects, or when ultrasound or a prenatal exam indicates a possible problem. The March of Dimes Foundation has invested millions of dollars in research to develop and expand the use of AFP. Other strong supporters of the procedure are the American College of Gynecologists and Obstetricians and the American Medical Association.

Opposition to AFP screening hinges on two concerns. First, the puncturing of the amniotic sac can cause miscarriage. Some research indicates that the rate of miscarriage associated with the procedure itself is as high as 20 percent, although most research indicates a rate closer to that of spontaneous pregnancy loss at sixteen weeks gestation. Second, AFP is often used to ferret out "defective" children. Ninety-eight percent of babies found to be defective through AFP and other confirmatory testing are aborted.

Another important consideration is the accuracy of the test. Whereas amniocentesis yields enough of a sample of amniotic fluid for cytogenetic analysis (the analysis of chromosomes for genetic defects) in nearly 99 percent of the procedures, the clinical interpretation of the results may not be conclusive. It is difficult for laboratories to differentiate between cytogenetic abnormalities that reflect true chromosomal defects and aberrations resulting from laboratory "pollutants."

Consequently, it is possible for normal, healthy preborns to be aborted because clinicians report an abnormality.

Chorion Villus Sampling (CVS)

CVS uses a transvaginal, transcervical or transabdominal biopsy of chorion villi to detect a variety of potential fetal deformities or defects. Chorion villi are part of the vascular embryonic membrane that forms part of the placenta. In early pregnancy the chorion villi provide some of the earliest genetic information about the human embryo.[1] Though the accuracy of CVS is comparable to that of AFP, the procedure involves a direct biopsy of fetal tissue, rather than a testing of shed fetal cells in the amniotic fluid. Most research indicates fetal loss at an average of one out of every two hundred CVS procedures when performed in conjunction with real time ultrasound.[2]

Perhaps the primary reason CVS was developed and has become so widely used is the fact that the procedure can be done much earlier in pregnancy. Amniocentesis AFP screening is done well into the second trimester. By the time the tissue culture grows and the test results are reported, a woman is visibly pregnant and has felt the baby move. Aborting a defective baby at that point in the pregnancy is very difficult. CVS allows a physician an earlier look at the unborn child and, if a defect is found, an earlier abortion for the mother, which is considered less threatening to her health.

Assuming CVS yields an accurate picture of fetal health, the "cure"—abortion—is unacceptable. Unfortunately, most babies found with (or thought to have) defects are aborted. For the most part they were planned children, wanted by their parents until the discovery that they were less than perfect.

Again, with CVS there is a potential for misdiagnosis and miscarriage. Many physicians advise patients of the test's availability in order to comply with the standards of care established by the American College of Obstetricians and Gynecologists (ACOG).

IMPLICATIONS FOR SOCIETY

The development and use of probes to assess overall genetic health of preborn children could lead us to consider parents irresponsible when they knowingly allow the birth of a handicapped child. Nancy Dubler, a physician at the Montefore Medical Center in New York City, contends, "There is the fundamental assumption that we as a society cannot make and enforce decisions. We as a society should have a reproductive policy which states that we should test for those conditions that are a burden to life to such a degree that it is permissible to exclude them."

Others join her in arguing that the real purpose of obstetrics is to produce "optimum babies," which is an unmitigated focus on quality control. It is not hard to see that the introduction of genetic screening into the procreation process was based upon eugenic premises. Genetic screening gives man the power to exclude those who do not fit the desired design.

Although required genetic testing for all pregnant women is not yet socially or politically feasible, if left unchecked, widespread reliance upon genetic screening could become mandatory, especially in a day of climbing health care costs. It could lead to a day when individuals with incompatible genotypes are prohibited from marrying or are required to be sterilized. Although those scenarios are extreme, they should not be ignored.

SUSCEPTIBILITY TESTING

What insurance company would not appreciate knowing whether a potential policy holder has a genetic predisposition to high blood pressure, diabetes, or other life-threatening, life-shortening conditions? What employer would not like to know if a prospective employee is prone to developing Parkinson's or will develop heart disease at age fifty? Probes to detect DNA markers for cystic fibrosis, sickle cell, Tay-Sachs disease, and other serious diseases could be used by insurance underwriters to screen applicants before offering them coverage. That does not seem far-fetched when we consider that employer-provided health coverage increasingly does not cover pre-existing conditions of new employees.

A further consideration is the prospect that companies will expand their pre-employment medical exams to include genetic screening to determine if a prospective employee is susceptible to illnesses or diseases linked to exposure to certain chemicals used by the company. Companies such as Du-Pont, Dow Chemical, and other manufacturers of chemicals already screen employees for genetic susceptibilities. The Occupational Health and Safety Act and other federal legislation have placed responsibility for employee safety squarely on the shoulders of industry, which is a powerful incentive for companies to protect themselves from regulatory agencies by screening out individuals who might be at risk.

However, if such a practice becomes widespread we may find ourselves in a society where the new discrimination is not race or color but genotype.

GENETIC THERAPY AND ENGINEERING

Suppose our expertise in human genetics someday matches that of organ transplants. What if gene technology develops to the point where we can not only detect but also correct a genetic defect with laser surgery or gene splicing? Imagine that we could use gene therapy to eliminate many genetic disorders without killing the carriers or preventing them from mating.

Most would regard such breakthroughs as monumental and would consider such technology highly beneficial. Yet might not such a "success" reflect an altered view of man and his role upon the earth? It has the potential to fulfill C. S. Lewis's vision of man succumbing to his own technology.

There is no guarantee that genetic technology will remain safely in the realm of treating medical disorders. Perhaps the technology that allows us to eliminate bad genes will also empower us to replace them with desired "designer" genes. Would we be tempted to try to eliminate racism by manipulating genes that determine skin color and other physical characteristics? Perhaps we could produce ten-foot-tall basketball players and eliminate dwarfism. Rather than considering such technology an aberration, perhaps we should embrace it, recognizing that man is functioning as image bearer and using his God-given talents.

However, it is one thing for man to exercise dominion over plants, animals, and other nonhuman creatures; it is quite another to exercise dominion over fellow man. It is one thing to engineer a new engine and quite another to engineer the engineer.

Cloning

In the book *In His Image*, David Rorvik describes a European industrialist who claimed to have successfully cloned himself. The claim has been denounced by the scientific community as a fraud, much as many wish it were true.

In theory, cloning involves the gestation of an unfertilized egg, a sort of "virgin birth." By employing the recombinant DNA technique, a DNA strand containing 46 chromosomes is spliced into a female ovum, and gestation is begun. The result would be a genetic duplicate of the person from whom the DNA was obtained.

Though the temptation exists to propose a moral response to cloning, the technology is so hypothetical that any moral analysis would be equally hypothetical.

Concerns About Genetic Therapy and Engineering

If we succeed in mapping the human genome and in developing therapies to correct genetic disorders, how will that affect the biblical view of man? Will it reshape our thinking about parenting? Who will control information about individual genotypes, and what will be done with the information? Who will decide what constitutes a defect? What criteria will be used in deciding which "defects" need to be eliminated?

It is crucial to recognize that there are legitimate uses of genetic engineering. For example, Interferon, an effective cancer-fighting drug, was produced through genetic engineering, as was the AIDS drug AZT. Increased growth for cattle has cut the cost of meat production. Genetically engineered insulin enables diabetics who are allergic to animal insulin to enjoy a better quality of life. The benefits of genetic engineering cannot be denied.

QUESTIONS TO THINK ABOUT

1. How can one determine whether a proposed medical treatment is of God or of man?
2. If you could clone someone, who would it be and why?
3. If you could use genetic engineering to eliminate any disease, which would you eliminate, and why?
4. If a technology is being used for evil purposes, does that mean no one can use it for good? Should we legislate against the immoral use of technology?

Part 4:

Issues in Death and Dying

9

EUTHANASIA

Whatever proportion these crimes [Nazi war crimes] finally assumed, it became evident to all who investigated them that they had started from small beginnings. The beginnings at first were merely a subtle shift in emphasis in the basic attitudes of physicians. It started with the acceptance of the attitude, basic in the euthanasia movement, that there is a life not worthy to be lived.

Dr. Leo Alexander, psychiatrist who helped draft the Nuremberg Code of Medical Ethics used in Nazi medical trials

CASE STUDY

Eighty-seven-year-old Helga Wanglie has been in a persistent vegetative state (PVS) since she suffered a massive heart attack two years ago. Her higher brain is not functioning and will ultimately liquify. She is totally unconscious, with no sensation or awareness. Her brain stem continues to function, so she does not meet the legal criteria for brain death. Major organs—kidneys, heart, liver—function on their own. Her lungs have weakened, however, so she has been placed on a ventilator.

Prior to her heart attack, Mrs. Wanglie prepared a living will stating that she wants everything done to sustain her life, a request her family intends to enforce. Her physicians argue that the respirator represents futile medical care, no longer achieving any reasonable medical goals.

You serve on the hospital's ethics committee that advises the staff physicians and hospital administration. Would removing Mrs. Wanglie from the respirator constitute killing her?

EUTHANASIA DEFINED

The term euthanasia has been defined a number of ways, the most common being "a good death," or a death relatively free of pain. It is most often used in connection with people who are terminally ill and desire to die rather than continue suffering.

In the debate surrounding euthanasia, two distinct concepts have evolved—passive and active euthanasia. I do not believe there is any relevant moral difference between the two. Passive euthanasia is the bringing about of death by not doing something, such as not continuing medical treatment. Thus the person is not killed by direct action but by deliberate neglect. In contrast, active euthanasia means directly killing an individual in order to eliminate further suffering. Active euthanasia is also called "mercy killing" since the motivation appears to be compassion toward the suffering person. It is active by virtue of the fact that specific actions are taken to end a life.

In both cases, the intent is to bring about death. Whether the means are active or passive is insignificant if the desired result is achieved. Is there really a difference between withholding medical treatment in order to bring about death and giving a lethal injection? Therefore, euthanasia can be defined as withholding or withdrawing treatment for the purpose of bringing about or hastening death, or taking specific, deliberate steps to end a life when that person is not imminently dying.

THE RIGHT TO DIE

Euthanasia has as its philosophical underpinning the notion of a right to die. The belief that every individual has the right to control his own life extends to his right to end it. In its modern form, the right to die means the right to death upon demand. In former days the right to die merely meant the right to die a "natural" death, without burdensome medical care.

In this age of cardiopulmonary resuscitation, ventilators, and other sophisticated means of life support, the prospect of overtreatment, of being kept alive "artificially," presents the average person with the possibility of experiencing a life he neither desires nor enjoys. Therefore, the right to die is asserted whereby resuscitation and life support can be withheld. The desire to die of "natural causes" rather than prolonging the process by technology is what most people mean when they talk about the right to die.

If a right to death upon demand does exist, one's health or life expectancy has little to do with the decision. Even a healthy individual would have the right to take his own life should life become intolerable. Yet the Judeo-Christian ethical tradition holds that that would be suicide, and self-murder is prohibited by the sixth commandment—"Thou shalt not kill."

Biblically, there are several arguments to be made against the claim for this right. First, God is sovereign, and He alone determines the length of days (1 Samuel 2:6; Psalm 39:4).

Second, a Christian does not own himself, for we have been purchased by God (1 Corinthians 6:19b-20). Since we do not own ourselves we have no right to dispose of ourselves. God determines when, where, and under what circumstances our lives will come to an end.

Third, to consider the right to die as an inalienable right enjoyed under the Constitution means that it should be self-evident and derived from a law higher than man's. How, then, do we explain Christianity's significant influence upon cultures, causing them to outlaw suicide, murder, and mercy killing? Assisted suicide has been considered a criminal offense for centuries. If anything is self-evident it is that murder, including self-murder, is wrong.

Fourth, physical life is intrinsically good, not merely a means to another good. Our bodies are not incidental to our existence; they are an integral aspect of our "being." If the body were not significant to being but merely "the tomb of the soul," as Plato described it, why would God bother to resurrect and glorify it? Why not just create an entirely new body or create beings with no body at all?

Since the body is important to our being and because bodily life is good, it is improper to speak of continued bodily life as a burden. If physical life is not inherently good, and if "to live is Christ, and to die is gain" (Philippians 1:21), why do we attempt to extend this earthly life? Why would any Christian go to a doctor? If this body is insignificant, why spend money trying to keep it healthy? We may not understand the purpose for our bodily existence on earth, but that does not mean that there is no purpose. We may not desire to live a life devoid of "quality," but the notion of quality of life is purely subjective and arbitrary. Few would desire a life sustained by locusts and honey, with sackcloth for dress, and a home in the wilderness, but aren't we grateful that John the Baptist lived that life? One of the consequences of belief in the sovereignty of God is accepting the fact He often chooses to do things differently than we would. Sometimes that may mean an earthly life characterized by deprivation and hardship.

On the other hand, the right to die may be legitimate if it means the right to refuse burdensome medical treatment when terminally ill, if such treatment is of little or no benefit. Traditional principles of medical ethics and the law recognize patient autonomy, which includes the right to refuse treatment. And individual autonomy is not entirely outside the biblical framework of man. Within the Christian theology we have a degree of autonomy in that we are divine image bearers, meaning we are rational, thinking beings to whom God grants the power to make certain decisions. Decision making is one of our most human traits. However, our autonomy to make decisions does not eliminate responsibility for the results of those choices.

A legal argument favoring the right to die might be made, under the definition that the individual, as opposed to the state, has a right to determine how his or her death should be managed. We should not give the state power to determine how and when its citizens die.

Inevitably, the issue is who has ultimate control over individual lives. We must be careful to remember that the ultimate claim to our lives belongs not to ourselves or the state but to God. Asserting the right to die is the logical extension of humanism, which holds that man is the center of all things. When we consider all of the control man assumes over the entrance gates of life it should come as no surprise that man will seek to extend that control to the exit gates of life as well.

Let's examine what modern technology has given us: Conception control to prevent wrongful conception. Failing that, abortion to prevent wrongful birth. Infanticide prevents wrongful life, and the "solution" to the wrongful burden of growing old is the right to die.

DEATH WITH DIGNITY

For the child of God, death means a departure from earthly life and an entrance into the presence of God for eternity (2 Corinthians 5:1-10). To be absent from the physical body is to be present with the Lord, the greatest hope of every believer. The psalmist declared, "Precious in the sight of the Lord is the death of His godly ones" (116:15). God looks forward to having His children with Him.

However, death itself is not dignified. It is an affront to dignity because it is the consequence of sin (Genesis 2:17). Every observance of death, whether it be a dead animal in the middle of the road or a human corpse in a funeral home, should remind us of the terrible price of rebellion against God. How can God's judgment against sin be considered dignified? Any effort to make it so is an attempt to hide the consequences of sin, thereby negating our need for Christ.

Proverbs 8:36 states, "All those who hate me [God] love death." How is death portrayed in modern culture? Popular music is filled with references to it. Nearly all the songs of a group called Suicidal Tendencies glorify death. It is no wonder that suicide is a leading cause of death among teenagers, reaching epidemic proportions.

The Bible teaches the existence of a literal hell—a place of eternal torment and separation from God for all who reject the Lord Jesus Christ (John 3:16; Revelation 14:10; 21:8). No matter how peaceful or controlled the surroundings, or how painless or welcome it may be, the death of an unbeliever is undignified because the only thing he can look forward to is judgment and separation from God.

It may be appropriate to speak of a believer's death as dignified if we mean that he or she experiences a peaceful homegoing, one relatively free from pain and suffering. The death of Francis Schaeffer, the great Christian philosopher-theologian, could properly be called dignified. Once it was determined that medicine offered no further extension of his life following a long battle with cancer, Schaeffer was released from the hospital and sent home. His death came shortly after he visited with each member of his family, while his favorite music played in the background.

Most Christians hope that their lives will end similarly, in the company of family and friends, in anticipation of a glorious entrance into the Lord's presence. By that definition, the concept of death with dignity is acceptable. However, we must remind ourselves that the event of death is never dignified.

IMMINENT DEATH

The term imminent death frequently refers to an individual's impending death. Christians speak of the imminent return of Christ, meaning He could return at any moment. When we connect the term to death, it means that death could happen at any time. Using the term this way it could apply to any living person, regardless of his health. All of us are imminently dying since we have no guarantee that we will live another minute.

However, when that term is applied to specific patients, it means that their death appears unavoidable and near, given their deteriorating medical condition. Usually that means death can be expected within hours or days. Many people have survived such dire predictions, which shows that the concept of imminent death is not definitive nor empirical.

Some in the euthanasia movement want to apply the term *imminent death* to a person diagnosed as terminally ill. Unfortunately, the phrase *terminal illness* suffers from the same ambiguities as the term _imminent death_. How certain is a particular diagnosis? Many have been told they had less than a year to live, only to survive for many more. Certainty is not the strong suit of medical diagnosis, even with sophisticated diagnostic tools and extensive studies of terminally ill patients.

When the terms _imminent death_ and _terminal illness_ are used, it should mean that from a consideration of all the medical data, patient examinations, and the relevant medical research, death appears to be unavoidable. If death appears to be unavoidable within six months, it is a terminal illness. If death appears unavoidable within hours or, at best, days, then death would be considered imminent.

ARTIFICIAL LIFE SUPPORT

Many people say they would not want to be kept alive by artificial means, which usually means they do not want machines performing the functions for which their major organs were designed. They assume that the medical apparatus is capable of sustaining lives indefinitely.

It should be understood that no amount of medical expertise or technology can keep a person alive indefinitely when there is no spontaneous major organ function. Organ systems function in an integrated manner. The loss of one major organ system affects the others. If all major organ systems cease functioning spontaneously and initial efforts at resuscitation are unsuccessful, no amount of technology can keep that person alive.

Significant changes have taken place in recent years in classifying what constitutes medical treatment. Some state courts have followed the lead of the New Jersey Supreme Court in classifying hydration and nutrition (fluids and food) as artificial medical treatment.

It should be noted that medical procedures often have several purposes, all related to treating illness, disease, or repairing injury. Medical therapies and procedures are usually applied to people with particular symptoms and pathologies. However, food and water have only one purpose—to physically sustain life, whether the person is sick or not. Even the healthiest person needs food and water to remain alive. It does not take a medical genius to understand that without nutrition and fluids anyone's prognosis is death. Therefore, food and water are not medical treatment—if they were, each of us would be receiving approximately three medical treatments every day without a doctor's prescription.

Courts have ruled in cases where individuals are sustained by "artificial feeding," meaning intravenous fluids or feeding tube. Numerous cases have been litigated, the most prominent being the U.S. Supreme Court case *Cruzan v. Director, Missouri Department of Health* (1990), which involved a woman who was permanently unconscious and being fed through a feeding tube. Nancy Cruzan's parents asked the court to allow the removal of the tube since it was artificial medical treatment.

It is true that the fluids, vitamins, and minerals kept her alive, but those were also the only things keeping the judges on the Supreme Court alive. Nancy breathed on her own, her heart beat on its own, and her kidneys filtered impurities out of her blood. The principal difference between Cruzan and a "normal" person was that she lacked consciousness due to severe brain damage following an auto accident. She had been diagnosed as being in a persistent vegetative state and had irreversible brain damage.

The medicalizing of food and water represents a radical departure from previous standards of care. Until recently, food and water were considered basic care, even when provided by IV or feeding tube. Nutrition cannot rightly be classified as artificial medical treatment. It is basic to continued life, without which no human being can survive. As such, to deliberately withhold food and water in order to hasten death is euthanasia or, more accurately, homicide. Death results from starvation and dehydration, not "natural causes."

Does oxygen fall into the same category as food and water? Would withdrawing a respirator be as unethical as withdrawing or withholding food and water?

If the purpose in removing the respirator is to hasten or bring about death, then it is wrong, just as it is wrong to withdraw or withhold food and water for the purpose of causing death. However, it is not wrong in every case, as will be explained later in this chapter.

Also known as ventilators, respirators have become an important part of intensive care and emergency room medicine. They are used for a variety of purposes, including maintaining oxygen flow for trauma victims, assisting breathing during major surgery, and helping imperiled infants born with underdeveloped lungs. Respirators are used to sustain a sufficient level of oxygen in the bloodstream in order to maintain the integrity of major organ systems.

There is no question that inserting a ventilator tube is uncomfortable. It limits a person's mobility, which may interfere with one's ability to engage in particular activities. However, in many instances the benefit far outweighs the burden.

When a person's medical condition deteriorates to the point where he is no longer able to breathe on his own and death appears imminent, does respirator support become artificial life support? In a strict sense, yes. A machine is maintaining a major organ function. However, the issue of removing the respirator is determined by the overall condition of the patient, not the nature of the machine. The fact that the machine is breathing for the patient has little to do with the ethics of respirators. When we fly in a commercial airliner we do not roll down a window at 30,000 feet and hang our heads out the window to get oxygen. The airplane is equipped with an "artificial" means of providing oxygen. The issue is not whether the means of providing oxygen is artificial but whether the machine is a benefit to the patient or not. The question to ask is, What is the individual's condition? Will he die soon, regardless of whether we provide oxygen or not?

Oxygen, like food and water, is not medical. It is basic to life. A healthy person will die when deprived of any of the three. It is inappropriate to speak of oxygen, food, or water as artificial. Only the means of delivering them to the body can be artificial.

WITHHOLDING OR WITHDRAWING TREATMENT

Many of the circumstances surrounding end-care medical decision making center on the issue of withdrawing or withholding treatment. Is it ever moral to take a person off a respirator, antibiotics, kidney dialysis, or insulin? Are we required to squeeze every possible moment out of life?

Death cannot be avoided. That is not a principle of medical ethics but a fact of life. People die every day, despite the advances of medicine. Death is not simply a technical matter involving the failure of the body to sustain life; it is a spiritual reality, as we have already discussed. God is ultimately in control, whether we choose to accept it or not.

Therefore, when medicine reaches its limits and can no longer sustain life, we must accept the fact that death will occur. That may mean choosing to withdraw a particular treatment or deciding not to begin a new one. Yet it is imperative that such decisions not be motivated by economic, social, or utilitarian reasons. Decisions concerning the withdrawal or withholding of treatment should be based primarily on the individual's physical condition. For example, decisions regarding a mentally disabled patient's treatment should not be affected by her disability. If the proposed procedure will benefit that particular patient, it should be done. Medical benefit should be the primary goal. Otherwise, we would be practicing eugenics.

Likewise, if a medical treatment would not benefit a patient, then it should not be instituted. Care givers often object to futile treatment when prospects for benefit are minimal or nonexistent. Perhaps a general rule of thumb is to ask, Will this patient leave the hospital alive if this particular therapy is provided? If the answer is no—if death is unavoidable—then a decision to withhold the therapy would not be euthanasia.

However, that does not mean that medical judgment is infallible. Diagnosis and treatment are nearly as much art as science. It is not unusual for a physician to attempt a treatment he is not positive will benefit a patient. When it does not benefit him or her or causes additional harm, the treatment is removed and replaced with another. Treating a particular patient may involve a series of attempts whose outcome is uncertain.

However, when treatment is withheld or withdrawn specifically to hasten or cause death, then the moral boundary of euthanasia has been crossed.

A growing number of people subscribe to the idea that an individual should be able to expect a certain quality of life. Usually that means a life of communication with people, meaningful relationships, participation in joys and struggles, and the ability to be self-directed and independent.

Therefore, when one is no longer capable of participating in that kind of life, the common response is that physical life should end. Right to die advocates contend that the essence of humanness is the integrated human activities we all enjoy. Bodily existence is just an instrument that enables us to participate in life. In other words, what really counts is not being alive but experiencing that life in relationship to other people. Consequently, when the capacity for rational and relational participation in the human community is no longer possible due to severe illness or injury, the person has lost his quality of life.

Those who do not experience this quality of life are typically referred to as "vegetables" or "vegetating organisms," implying that physical existence alone is not human. Such people who occupy beds in nursing homes or other long-term care facilities and are fed through feeding tubes but exhibit no signs of sapient life are considered candidates for feeding tube removal by an increasing cadre of care givers. As discussed earlier, the suggested withdrawal is premised on the assumption that a feeding tube is artificial life support and that merely maintaining physical existence is not providing a benefit.

We are not just talking about the terminally ill or imminently dying. Those affected are people whose biological tenacity presents society with a problem—they are not dying fast enough. Although the proponents of euthanasia view such lives as useless, many care givers are understandably wary of hastening anyone's death.

It should be restated that it is not always wrong to withdraw or withhold a feeding tube. There are instances when feeding a person is just as futile as attempting cardiopulmonary resuscitation. I am not advocating that every person in every situation be provided with the full application of our medical expertise in order to squeeze a few extra moments into this earthly life. When is it acceptable to remove a feeding tube?

- When the person is no longer capable of benefiting from continued feeding
- When continued feeding would increase the suffering of an imminently dying person (one who will die within hours or days)
- When the purpose for withdrawing or withholding nutrition is to make the person more comfortable, not to hasten or cause death
- When the person's family or advocate agrees to the decision

All of those criteria must be met, especially the last two points.

Sometimes patients in the advanced stages of colon cancer develop blockages exacerbated by feeding. Feeding them increases pain. Such patients do not usually have a sensation of hunger because the pain medication eliminates appetite. To withhold or withdraw tube feeding from such a patient would not be euthanasia.

What about removing a person from a respirator? Is removing a respirator from someone who is not imminently dying euthanasia? Yes, if the person is benefiting from the respirator and the only reason for removing it is to bring about death. However, when it is clear that death is near because the other major organ systems are shutting down, to remove a respirator would not be euthanasia. When all brain function has ceased it will not be long before the other organ systems begin to deteriorate.

One distinction should be made between removing a respirator and removing a feeding tube. Breathing, unlike eating, is an involuntary act. We do not choose to breathe as we choose to eat. We cannot select which air to breathe; we must breathe whatever air is available. However, we do choose which food to eat and when to eat it. We can choose not to eat for such a period of time that we lapse into unconsciousness and ultimately die. In contrast, although one may choose to hold his breath for such a period of time that he becomes unconscious, once unconscious he will immediately resume breathing (unless he is underwater). The act of eating is associated with consciousness, thought, emotion—all higher brain functions. Breathing is similar to blood circulation, digestion, and kidney function in that they are involuntary brain stem functions.

The central issue concerning respirators is whether or not they provide the patient the benefit intended. That is a strict medical issue. Is the machine providing oxygen that is benefiting the patient's major organs? Whether the patient can afford the respirator and the quality of life she may or may not have are immaterial. If the respirator is not providing any benefit to the patient's physical integrity and she will not survive even with its support, then its removal would not be the cause of death.

I want to emphasize that respirators do not keep people alive. People die on respirators all the time because no amount of sophisticated medical machines can keep an individual alive where there exists no spontaneous organ function and where organ integrity has been destroyed.

DO NOT RESUSCITATE ORDERS

I have attempted to address some of the issues related to end-care medical decision making, particularly as they relate to euthanasia. In repudiating euthanasia we do not endorse the practice of continuing futile medical treatment or multiple resuscitations just to extract a few more moments or days of earthly life.

At times one can justify not using technology. The fact that a technology exists and works does not mean it is moral. Although a number of clinical variations can occur, generally speaking when a person suffers multiple cardiac arrests in succession, further resuscitative efforts may be withheld.

Such an order may be written on his medical chart or, in the case of a terminally ill person who is at home, he may wish to indicate to emergency medical technicians or others that he does not wish to be resuscitated.

CONCLUSION

If anything is certain it is that man will continue to push for greater longevity. We will continue to be confronted by further efforts to push the limits of earthly life. Decision making at the exit gates of life will become more complex and ethically demanding.

Christians must lead in the midst of the medical schizophrenia that pervades modern medicine. The world should be able to look to Christians for guidance on such issues as death and dying.

QUESTIONS TO THINK ABOUT

1. Is quality of life more important than sanctity of life?
2. What is an acceptable quality of life? Is there such a thing as a life not worthy of being lived?
3. If a person is permanently unconscious, as far as a medical examination is able to determine, would it be moral to remove a feeding tube?
4. Is there a moral difference between passive and active euthanasia?
5. What biblical teachings might be used against "mercy killing"?

10

ASSISTED
SUICIDE

An ethics committee is consulted on the case of a fifty-year-old woman who has been afflicted with multiple sclerosis for approximately fifteen years. Over that time she gradually became more and more dependent, eventually requiring a wheelchair. She often did not have the strength to complete even simple tasks. She had been depressed for several years about her physical deterioration and had received psychiatric attention, but it did not cure her depression. Her psychiatrist's opinion was that she was still competent to make her own medical decisions.

She had already attempted suicide by an overdose. She was treated and released. Her second attempt a year later has brought her back to the hospital. She is now unconscious and dependent on a respirator. Cranial nerve reflexes are present, and she is not brain dead; there has not yet been time for the drugs to be cleared from her system.

A month ago she executed a "living will" in which she directed her physicians not to use artificial means to "only prolong her dying" if she became irreversibly ill. She also named her husband as her proxy decision maker to interpret her wishes if unable to do so for herself. In a separate document she granted him durable power of attorney to make all personal and financial decisions for her. Her husband, backed by her daughter, now demands that the respirator be removed in accordance with her living will and her well-documented wish to die. He points out that if she were to recover, she would be in a state that she considers intolerable. Furthermore, it is likely that she would not recover fully but would be even more impaired, if the respirator is maintained.

The attending physician believes that he cannot withdraw the respirator since her coma and respiratory depression may be due to the effects of the drugs. He believes that acceding to the family's wishes would be assisting the patient's suicide, which he cannot do in good conscience. What counsel would you offer the physician and the patient's family?

Other doctors would seem to have fewer scruples. Retired pathologist Jack Kervorkian, nicknamed "Dr. Death" in medical school for his bizarre proposals for using organs from convicted criminals and his obsession with death, participated in the deaths of three women in Michigan, none of whom was terminally ill. One woman in the early stages of Alzheimer's disease was hooked up to his "suicide machine" in the back of his van. A second woman had multiple sclerosis, similar to our case study, and the third had chronic vaginal pain. All three requested help in ending their lives, although each was capable of committing suicide without his assistance.

Suicide, by definition, is self-murder and is proscribed by the sixth commandment—"Thou shalt not kill." Every suicide in the Bible is cast in a negative light. *Self-deliverance*, the term preferred by pro-euthanasia groups such as the Hemlock Society, is as morally offensive as murder in that it is a rejection of God's sovereign rule of every person. Suicide is the ultimate demonstration of control.

In Genesis 3, an important aspect of Satan's deception of Eve is his insistence that she will not die if she eats from the forbidden tree. God told her that if she ate the fruit she would die. Satan's ploy was to convince her that if she ate from that tree she would gain control, in this case of knowledge, and she would learn that God had lied. Satan's enticement was to power over death.

The enticement of suicide is a similar satanic seduction to power. He attempts to deceive us into believing that death is a release and a legitimate means to avoid suffering. Rather than submit to the lordship of Christ and rest in the knowledge that He will not allow us to suffer more than we are able, that He has promised that everything will work for the good of the child of God, we are tempted by Satan to seize control and destroy ourselves.

Assisted suicide is a misnomer. If one needs assistance to commit suicide, it is no longer "self-inflicted" death. If an individual participates in a murder, he is considered an accessory. In assisted suicide the one who assists is an accessory, a fact that laws related to suicide have always recognized. Assisting someone to die is not suicide—it is homicide.

When killing is done to end suffering, it is frequently called mercy killing. Relief from suffering, not malice, is the principal motivation, although relief from watching a loved one suffer may be a secondary motive. Mercy killing implies that death is preferable to life. It also assumes that no other form of relief is available. Yet of all the advances in modern medicine, the management of chronic pain seems to have progressed the furthest. Not all pain can be completely controlled, but there is no reason for most people to suffer intense, ongoing pain and discomfort.

However, in managing pain another problem is created. A physician may prescribe morphine to reduce the pain of a terminally ill cancer patient, knowing that that painkiller will actually shorten the person's life. Does that mean he is killing his patient? No, because he would not be ordering morphine to manage pain if the person were not suffering from cancer. The underlying illness kills the patient, not the painkiller. The painkiller is intended to manage pain, not kill.

No one drives to work for the purpose of wearing rubber off his tires. Yet such wearing is one result of operating a vehicle. Likewise, providing painkilling medication may shorten a terminally ill person's lifespan, but that is not the purpose of administering the drugs. That is not mercy killing. But if a physician administers dosages beyond the amount needed to manage pain, that becomes mercy killing, or murder. If 50 mg of morphine are required to control pain but 500 mg are administered, that is an obvious intent to bring about death.

Most proposals to change state laws concerning assisted suicide focus on requests from competent patients. The assumption is that someone who wants to end his life is mentally competent, but existing law contradicts that claim. People who fail in their suicide attempts are generally admitted to hospitals for psychiatric care, because society thinks that a mentally healthy person would not want to die. Assisted suicide claims just the opposite.

A proposal to legalize assisted suicide (Initiative 119) in Washington state was defeated in November 1991. The proposal's wording provided insight into what pro-euthanasia advocates ultimately want. During the campaign, supporters admitted that the right of a terminally ill, competent person to request physician assistance in dying would also apply to an incompetent person. If measures like that are adopted, physicians will be allowed, perhaps obligated, to administer lethal injections to patients whom they believe would want to die if able to make the decision themselves. Washington voters recognized the implications—physician-administered death would compromise the integrity of the medical profession.

Physician-assisted and physician-administered death are already widespread in the Netherlands, where one of every six deaths is the result of a doctor-administered lethal injection. In the early stages, the practice was limited to terminally ill patients who requested it. Now it is common for lethal injections to be administered to unconscious or incompetent patients. Although the practice is technically illegal, Dutch authorities do not enforce laws prohibiting it.

Ironically, those Dutch physicians are doing what their World War II counterparts refused to do during the Nazi occupation of the Netherlands. In his book *The Nazi Doctors*, Robert J. Lifton describes how the Dutch medical community resisted Nazi orders to hand over patient records and participate in exterminative medicine. None cooperated. Many were sent to concentration camps for their refusal, but the doctors remained adamant. Just forty-eight years later their successors are making the choices that they so heroically resisted under an oppressive, totalitarian government. The medical ethic so clearly repudiated at Nuremberg has been socially rehabilitated in the Netherlands. And it's finding sympathizers in the U.S.

Life can be burdensome in many ways. Suffering is common to mankind because we live in a fallen world. It is the physician's role to eliminate suffering as well as he can, but it is not his role to eliminate the sufferer when relief cannot be found. We must not give physicians the legal or moral authority to decide who lives or dies. We must not grant them immunity to dispatch patients whom they are not capable of healing.

QUESTIONS TO THINK ABOUT

1. How would you handle the case detailed at the beginning of this chapter?
2. Do we have a moral obligation to keep an individual from taking his or her own life?
3. What does the Bible teach about suffering? Use Job as an example.

11

ADVANCE DIRECTIVES FOR HEALTH CARE

A dvance Directive" is the generic term for any document spelling out a person's wishes concerning how his or her death is to be managed. Such a document is often called a "living will." What makes the document unique is that it is anticipatory, made well in advance of the implementation of the patient's directions.

As we have seen, medical decision making is becoming increasingly complex. Rarely is anyone required to make one medical decision; usually he must make multiple choices. How are care givers to know a patient's wishes and values when he or she is unable to participate in the decision making due to advanced illness, traumatic injury, or unconsciousness?

Advance directives are a proposed means for making those wishes and values known to care givers, thereby reducing the potential for overtreating the patient and overburdening family members with difficult decisions. However, some advance directives are more harmful than helpful.

LIVING WILLS

A living will outlines an individual's wishes in general terms, often using language that is vague and open to a variety of interpretations. Many physicians indicate that patients are better off without one, and some states do not recognize them as binding. Consequently, some doctors ignore them. One problem is that no one can foresee all of the particulars relating to a future illness or injury. How can anyone really know what he or she would want done in case of cancer, stroke, or heart attack five or ten years before it occurs? Perhaps treatments will be developed that do not exist when the living will is drafted.

A second problem with a living will is that it names no one to make unforeseen medical decisions for the person. If medical decisions that are not spelled out in the living will arise, physicians are faced with seeking a family member or having a conservator or guardian appointed by the courts. And the conservator's decisions may or may not be consistent with the patient's values.

DURABLE POWER OF ATTORNEY FOR HEALTH CARE

The durable power of attorney for health care often includes not only a declaration of the patient's values and wishes, but it also grants legal authority to another person to make medical decisions in her stead. Often the proxy is a family member, although nonrelatives can be appointed.

The proxy's responsibility is to make medical decisions consistent with the patient's expressed desires and values. When those desires or values are not explicitly stated, the proxy makes decisions deemed to be in the best interest of the patient.

Such a document is viewed as essential in this age of powerful medical technology. Many people fear one day being hooked up to machines while family members look on helplessly as the medical bills mount. In an age of "can do" medicine, the fear of overtreatment seems valid. Add to that the litigious nature of our society that leads doctors to order duplicate or unnecessary tests and other procedures in order to avoid malpractice claims, and you have a climate ripe for the abuse people fear.

DANGERS OF ADVANCE DIRECTIVES

The legal basis for advance directives is the right to die, or the right to demand death. As discussed in the chapter on euthanasia, the child of God does not have that right, at least not in a moral sense. Unless one states clearly in an advance directive what he believes about God and the authority of Scripture, it will be assumed that the final authority rests with the individual.

Another potential danger is the vague terminology that fails to represent the true wishes of the patient. As pointed out in previous discussions of euthanasia, the terms of artificial life support, terminal illness, imminent death, and so on are not precise, nor is there universal consensus regarding what they entail.

Perhaps the most difficult aspect of advance directives is the issue of substitute judgment. Many times in life it is harmless for someone else to make a decision for you. However, in other situations no one else but you can make the right decision. You cannot appoint someone else to make your marriage vows or cast your vote in a public election. Those choices not only require personal consent but contemporaneous consent, consent at the moment the choice is made. How can we be less careful in matters pertaining to life and death?

Considering the current legal climate concerning medical decision making, a Christian should have a protective advance directive that reflects biblical values and provides as much protection from medical neglect as any piece of paper can.

Below is an example of a protective medical decisions declaration developed by Baptists for Life.

PROTECTIVE MEDICAL DECISIONS DECLARATION

Values History and Declaration

This values history serves as a set of specific values-based directives for various medical interventions. It is to be used only in health care situations where I am unable to participate in making my own medical decisions and where my preferences concerning medical care are relevant. I direct that this values history and Protective Medical Decisions Declaration (PMDD) be made part of my medical record. A check and my initials beside each value indicates my beliefs and desires.

1. God, as revealed in the Bible, is sovereign, and He alone determines the length of my life.
2. The Bible is my source of final authority and all decisions in life must be consistent with its teachings.
3. Physical death for the child of God is only a departure from this earthly existence into the presence of God.
4. Life can be burdensome in many ways. However, no matter how burdened it may be, human life remains intrinsically good. Therefore, remaining alive is never to be rightly regarded as a burden, and deliberate killing of innocent human life is never to be rightly regarded as rendering a benefit.
5. Whereas the elimination of pain and/or suffering is one legitimate goal of medicine, bringing about the death of a human being to achieve it is not legitimate medical practice. Therefore, I reject the notion that providing aid in dying or assisted suicide is a legitimate role for physicians.
6. As a person, whether conscious or unconscious, I have a right not to be killed by those whose responsibility it is to provide medical care.
7. Although I do not wish to suffer great pain, I do not authorize anyone to carry out any action for the purpose of ending my life.
8. Since food and water are basic substances for physical existence, I authorize their withdrawal only when the following criteria have been met:
   a. when, in the best medical judgment, my death will occur within a matter of hours or days;
   b. when the intent is not to hasten my death but to provide additional relief from pain and physical suffering;
   c. when my appointed advocate(s) have given written consent;
   d. when it has been indicated on my medical record that the withdrawal of food and water does not mean the withdrawal of pain medication or other means of comfort care;

      e. when my physical condition has deteriorated to the point where I am no longer able to assimilate hydration and nutrition.

9. I DO / DO NOT wish to donate my major organs.

10. I authorize the administration of pain medication with the understanding that in attempting to control pain my life may be shortened.

11. Upon my death I want my body to be treated with respect.

12. Under the conditions listed below I wish to undergo cardiopulmonary resuscitation: _____.

13. Under the conditions listed below I want to be placed on a ventilator:
      a. In all circumstances
      b. For a trial period to determine effectiveness using reasonable medical judgment
      c. Under no circumstances. Explanation: _____.

14. I want to have all medications used for the treatment of my illness continued provided such medication continues to be physically beneficial.

15. I authorize the use of ☐ nasogastric, ☐ gastronomy, or ☐ other enteral feeding tubes to facilitate my medical and/or comfort care.

16. I authorize being placed on a dialysis machine under the following conditions:
      a. Under all circumstances where such treatment would be beneficial to my physical condition
      b. For a trial period of _____
      to determine effectiveness using reasonable medical judgment
      c. Under no circumstances. Explanation: _____.

17. I DO / DO NOT authorize an autopsy to determine the cause of my death.

18. I want to be admitted to the Intensive Care Unit under the following conditions: _____

19. If I am residing in a long-term care facility and experience a life-threatening change in my health status, I want 911 called in case of a medical emergency.

20. If I have been diagnosed as being terminally ill (death will most likely occur within one year), I do not wish to be resuscitated by emergency medical personnel.

21. If I am pregnant at such time as I am unable to make my own medical decisions, all efforts must be undertaken to maximize survival for me and my unborn child.

Additional Instructions

Because it is impossible to foresee specific circumstances under which someone else may have to make health care decisions for me, and since it is not possible for me to know what specific decisions I might make in those circumstances, I have seriously and carefully considered the principles and beliefs on which I base decisions for myself. The above values and instructions are intended to direct those whom I have named to make medical decisions for me should I be rendered unable to do so.

I direct my advocate(s) and all those involved with my medical care to follow the above instructions. These instructions are binding not only on my appointed advocate(s) but on any and all health care personnel or institutions which shall have responsibility for my health and life.

I, _____, being of sound mind, willfully and voluntarily make this declaration as a directive to be followed by anyone and everyone involved in my medical care at such time as I am unable to participate in my own medical decision making. I hereby designate and appoint _____ as my advocate/surrogate/attorney-in-fact (herein after called "advocate") to make health care decisions for me.

I understand that I may revoke or amend this declaration at any time.

My advocate is authorized to choose the appropriate course of treatment or nontreatment for me according to the instructions I have given.

The above named person has reviewed this declaration and values history and has agreed to serve as my advocate in full accord with my wishes.

My advocate has full power and authority to make health care decisions for me and this declaration is intended to confer immunity on my advocate unless it is determined that my advocate is not acting in accordance with my instructions. It is not intended to confer immunity on any physician, health care provider, or health care institution acting negligently or in bad faith.

If a guardian or conservator is to be appointed for me, I nominate my advocate as named in this declaration to serve as my guardian or conservator of my person.

Advocate Statement of Acceptance

I, _____, do hereby accept the appointment of _____ to serve as his/her advocate for medical decisions. I have discussed this declaration with the declarant and agree to comply to the best of my ability with its provisions and instructions.

By signing here I indicate that I understand the purpose and effect of this declaration and that I am a legal adult of at least eighteen years of age. I am a legal resident of the United States of America.

Signature of Declarant _____

Date _____

Signature of Advocate _____

Date _____

If the person named as my advocate is unavailable or unable to act as my agent, I appoint _____ as my alternate advocate.

Signature of Alternate _____

Date _____

Witnesses

I declare that the person who signed this document is personally known to me. I further declare that he/she signed or acknowledged this durable power of attorney for health care in my presence, and that he/she appears to understand

144

the document and to be under no duress, fraud, or undue influence. I am not the person appointed as an advocate by this declaration, nor am I the signer's health care provider or an employee of the signer's health care provider.

I declare that I am at least eighteen years of age and am a legal resident of the United States of America.

I declare that I am not related to the declarant by blood, marriage, or adoption and, to the best of my knowledge, I am not entitled to any part of his/her estate under a will now existing or by operation of law.

Signature of First Witness _____

Date _____

Signature of Second Witness _____

Date _____

Notarization may be required in some states.

INSTRUCTIONS FOR SIGNED DOCUMENTS

1. Keep a signed original with your other important papers in a secure place.
2. Give signed originals to your advocate, physician, family, pastor, and a close friend.
3. Discuss this document with your primary care physician, pastor, family, and any other people who would be affected by it.
4. Request that this document become part of your medical record.
5. Notify all holders of your PMDD declaration if you amend or revoke your instructions. A complete PMDD is available by writing Baptists for Life, Inc., P.O. Box 3158, Grand Rapids, MI 49501. Enclose $1.00 with your request.

12

THE ALLOCATION AND RATIONING OF HEALTH CARE

Mr. Thompson is sixty-eight years old and in the intensive care unit at City Hospital. He has been saved from death six times in the past eighteen months, each time receiving massive transfusions to replace the blood lost in his abdomen as a result of alcoholic liver disease. In addition, he has cancer of the esophagus, which could cause his death within a few months.

His problem is fairly common in ICUs. This is the thirty-seventh day of intensive care for this hospitalization. In the past eighteen months his ICU stays total ninety-eight days, resulting in a hospital bill in excess of $300,000, much of which has been paid by Medicare. Each hospitalization was precipitated by a period of heavy drinking.

Would it be wrong to limit Mr. Thompson to three hospitalizations for gastrointestinal bleeding due to alcoholism? After three hospital stays would it be morally permissible to provide only comfort care and allow him to die? Would you endorse the following moral judgment: "People who abuse their health have less claim on expensive life-prolonging medical care than those who have taken good care of themselves"?[1]

How would your judgment concerning Mr. Thompson change if there were only nine beds in the ICU and he was among three patients waiting for the ninth bed? What criteria should determine who occupies the last available bed?

IS THERE A NEED TO RATION HEALTH CARE?

Health care costs Americans more than $600 billion annually, nearly 13 percent of the Gross National Product. Whereas the cost of other goods and services has increased in single digits in the past ten years, the cost of health care is three times what it was five years ago. For example, in 1990 General Motors spent more money on health care for its employees than it spent on steel to make automobiles.

Several factors contribute to this situation. The duplication of services, waste, excessive paperwork, malpractice costs, and the expensive nature of research and development of new drugs and machines all affect the cost to the consumer. However, it does not appear that eliminating waste and duplication or that changing medical malpractice would significantly reduce the rapidly rising cost of health care. Perhaps the major determining factor in the cost of health care is the increasing demand for more and better care. Americans have come to expect miracles from modern medicine, creating health care into a consumer product like soft drinks, videos, or cars. Another factor is the increased demand for care resulting from careless living. In other words, sin (the greed of doctors and insurance companies and the recklessness of patients) is the leading reason for skyrocketing health care costs. People live as they please and expect medicine to fix the consequences.

There is a growing belief in society that health care rationing is inescapable; no amount of effort to eliminate waste and inefficiency in the health care system will change this fact. Rationing has already begun in Oregon, where a basic standard of medical care is guaranteed to all citizens. However, that means that the overall standard is lowered in order to accommodate greater numbers of people, particularly those not covered by private insurance.

THE RIGHT TO HEALTH CARE

Given the current emphasis upon individual rights and personal autonomy, it is not surprising that the claim to a right to health care has secured a strong hold on the public consciousness. Health care is considered morally special, unlike other commodities in society. The inability to pay should not exclude anyone from receiving treatment, particularly if we value individual human life.

But others believe that no one should receive what she cannot pay for; that to appropriate someone else's money to pay for one's own health care constitutes theft. Human life, according to this view, is not priceless, and there are limits to what society ought to spend on saving or extending life through medical intervention. Those who hold this view say it is immoral to take other people's money to give expensive life-extending care to someone who cannot pay for it herself. Supposedly it is wrong to take $300,000 from the health care pool in a health maintenance organization to provide an extra six months of life for a patient dying from AIDS contracted by homsexual activity. The latter view holds that not all human life is worthy of maximal efforts at preservation. The quality of life supersedes the sanctity of life. Therefore, an AIDS patient has less claim to health care resources than someone with heart disease. The principle supporting this view is justice. Health resources are finite. For whom should they be reserved? Who decides who receives which resources? Our society maintains no consensus of justice, so the answer is left to the most vocal and the most organized, which is hardly just. The majority may win, but the majority may not be right.

It may be that the principle of justice is a better approach to health care allocation than an emphasis upon autonomy, or individual rights. We see the principle of justice at work in other arenas. All of us have a limited right to police and fire protection, whether we pay taxes or not. We are protected by the military from foreign attack regardless of whether we pay income taxes. That is because society values human life highly enough to assume that we all deserve protection. However, that right is not absolute, because it would be impossible to provide universal twenty-four-hour police and fire protection unless the nation were transformed into a police state. One's claim to police or fire protection increases as the threat increases. It is impossible to provide an armed guard for every citizen since resources are finite. But if an intruder enters your home and threatens your life, your claim to police protection increases dramatically. A person receiving death threats has more of a claim to police protection than someone whose neighbor's dog is barking. The greater the threat, the greater the claim—all based upon a principle of justice.

If we accept the premise that health resources are finite, perhaps their allocation may be determined according to the same concept of justice. Under this principle neither caregivers nor patients would be able to make unlimited demands on hospitals or other public resources, especially in regard to futile or marginally beneficial or purely elective medical procedures. Tummy tucks, face lifts, and nontherapeutic cosmetic surgeries may be limited or eliminated altogether in order for those resources to be used in a more just manner. Likewise, organ transplants, fertility treatments, or other expensive life-extending treatments that offer only marginal prospect of benefit to a patient may also be limited or eliminated in order for medical resources to be offered to someone who could receive more benefit from them.

Given the depravity of man, it is difficult for individuals to make fair allocation decisions about their own health care, especially if they are poor or prone to poor health. It is also hard to imagine caregivers making completely just allocation decisions, even within the confines of a national health insurance program. Although the aim of socialized medicine is to provide basic health care for everyone, its effect is that the standard of health care is reduced. Yet, the wealthy can always circumvent the standard, as evidenced by the number of Canadian citizens who cross the border for certain kinds of health care because they cannot obtain it under their country's national health insurance program.

Therefore, using justice as the dominant ethical principle in allocating health care resources may create more problems than it solves. We must also bear in mind that socialized medicine, which adheres to a principle of justice, means that informed consent becomes less important. The predominant issue under socialized systems is whether the state will pay for it, not whether the patient agrees to it.

A CHRISTIAN VIEW OF HEALTH

Holding to the sanctity of human life does not necessarily mean we automatically treat human life as priceless. We more often behave as though the opposite were true: we drive at high speeds, eat improperly, don't get enough sleep, engage in rigorous sports, and so on. If we truly believed human life were priceless, we would be far more protective of our bodies than we are.

What is an acceptable life span? Is there such a thing as premature death? Are other things just as important as good health? A Christian view of health must address these issues.

The issue of longevity has plagued man since the Fall. How long should a person expect to live? Scripture speaks of seventy years as being a good life, which some take to mean that death before one's seventieth birthday is premature. If that is true, the Lord Jesus died prematurely. If you'd been around in Methuselah's day, death at seventy would have been considered premature. Obviously, life span is relative.

A casual reading of the gospels reveals that good health is something men have always sought and which Jesus endorsed with His extensive healing ministry. However, good health is only one good among many. Job illustrates that the greater good is to worship God, regardless of our physical condition (Job 2:9-10). He asked his wife rhetorically, "Shall we indeed accept good from God and not accept adversity?" Do we only worship and serve God when He showers us with blessing, or do we worship Him when bad things happen as well?

Scripture provides abundant counsel which, if heeded, will enhance one's health. Proverbs speaks of the ill effects of alcoholic beverages, illicit sexual relations, anger, worry, and overeating. Paul admonishes us to glorify God with our bodies. And studies of lifestyles reveal that those who do not drink, smoke, exhibit outbursts of anger, engage in sex with multiple partners, or overeat enjoy much better health and live longer than those who engage in such behaviors.

Generally Scripture urges moderation in all things since man is more than just his body. The human body is the temple of the Holy Spirit (1 Corinthians 6:19) and does not belong to us. Whether we eat or drink we are to glorify God (10:31). Maintaining one's health is an implicit part of fulfilling our scriptural obligations.

In order to fulfill that responsibility and to demonstrate a consistent sanctity of human life ethic, how much health care should a Christian expect? Does Christian stewardship affect health care? Some might afford sophisticated health care, just as they can afford an expensive home, but is that an exercise of good stewardship?

Many American Christian families could probably afford to drive a Rolls Royce provided they did nothing else. Driving an expensive car may require the sacrifice of other things, such as housing, food, and clothing. Whereas driving a fancy automobile may be enjoyable, there are other good choices to consider. One may be able to afford the Cadillac version of health care if willing to forgo other goods. Or one could accept the Chevrolet version, which might mean a shorter earthly life but may allow for the enjoyment of other things. It is difficult to determine on purely biblical grounds what constitutes an acceptable level of health care since none who lived during biblical times had access to the kind of health care we have available to us.

In former days the role of medicine consisted mainly of providing comfort care for the sick or dying, with limited ability to control certain diseases. Surgeries as routine as the removal of an inflamed appendix were unheard of until the time of penicillin and anesthesia, which meant that until then many Christians died "prematurely." The problem then was not a relative scarcity of health care resources but an absolute scarcity—they simply did not exist. Our problem now is that we are capable of doing much to extend life, and that has created an insatiable demand.

A Christian should seek a level of health that will provide for the enjoyment of a "normal" life span, keeping in mind that God is sovereign and can choose to end our lives before or after that time. Likewise, sin can result in death (Acts 5:4-5, 9) or illness (1 Corinthians 11:30). Christians should live according to biblical principles for personal behavior and temperament, fearing God and considering any length of life as a blessing from the Lord.

WHAT CONSTITUTES MEDICAL NEED?

Medical needs may be categorized in the following manner:

1. Immediate life-threatening injuries.

This would involve the kind of injuries most emergency units are designed to deal with—injuries from auto accidents, gunshot wounds, and so on. Those traumas demand immediate and intense attention, much the same as an intruder in your home would warrant a serious claim to police protection.

2. Immediate life-threatening disease or sickness.

This category would include such conditions as heart attack, stroke, various forms of meningitis, leukemia, and other cancers. If a person's life is threatened by the onset of disease or sickness, that is a valid claim to health care.

3. Medical deficiencies of particular limbs or organs that render the person incapable of functioning as he or she should.

Nearly all non–life-threatening medical conditions could be placed in this category. It may involve a broken leg, a laceration, bladder infection, or other manageable illness. Generally, emergency cases would be handled ahead of such conditions.

AGE AS A STANDARD IN ALLOCATING HEALTH CARE

Daniel Callahan, director of the Hastings Center in New York, advocates age as a valid barometer for allocating health care.[2] His criteria are:

1. After a person has lived out a natural life span (somewhere between seventy and eighty years), medical care should no longer be oriented toward resisting death.
2. Provision for those who have lived a natural life span will be limited to the relief of suffering.
3. The existence of medical technologies capable of extending the lives of the elderly who have lived a natural life span creates no presumption whatsoever that the technologies must be used for that purpose.

A growing number agree with Callahan, and some accuse him of not going far enough. Francis Crick claims that we should adopt a mandatory death law that takes effect upon one's eightieth birthday.

Some argue that the idea of medical need changes each time a new technology is developed. For example, no one ever "needed" an organ transplant until the development of solid organ substitution techniques. No one required a CAT scan until that technology became available, just as people in the1800s didn't need electricity to run their appliances, because they didn't have electrical appliances. Therefore, medical need alone is highly unreliable as a criteria for allocating health care. Likewise, age is unreliable since age is merely a number. Some people well into their eighties have better health than others in their fifties. A growing number reach their hundredth birthday in good health.

ECONOMICS AS A STANDARD
FOR ALLOCATING HEALTH CARE

Until recently, physicians controlled most health care resources and were free to allocate them for their patients' use. Today, many health care resources are controlled by large corporations, with physicians acting as mere employees. Consequently, physicians are in the unique position of appropriating other people's resources for their patients, whether the patients have the ability to pay for them or not.

As mentioned earlier, some would call that a form of theft—a type of "benevolent" expropriation or redistribution of wealth. Another negative feature is this: in taking away physicians' ability to allocate resources for their patients, the physician is no longer an uncompromised advocate for the patient's best interests. By forcing doctors to seek approval to use resources, we subject them to the whims of bureaucratic cost-cutting policies and cumbersome decision-making procedures.

If economics are to be the sole standard for allocating medical care, health care will become simply another part of a market economy of goods and services. That will work against the likelihood of maintaining a strong sanctity of life ethic. Whether a person is able to receive treatment or not is determined by the size of his wallet or the benevolence of various charitable organizations.

It should be noted that the tremendous cost of health care is, at least in part, due to the fact that higher prices are already charged those with the ability to pay in order to cover the costs of those who can't. If access to health care were determined solely by one's ability to pay, it is possible that costs would decrease somewhat; however, it would hardly make up for the society's loss in those who would die for lack of medical care. Unlike other consumer products, medical care is morally special; it cannot be compared with owning a car or home. The ability to pay cannot be the lone factor in allocating health care resources.

MEDICAL NEED AND THE PROBLEM OF SIN

Some of the most vigorous advocates of legal abortion and euthanasia are vocal in their castigation of legislators who enact laws that impinge on the perceived "freedom to choose" and "right" to privacy, but in the very next breath they want government to fund such choices. Many strong advocates of abortion and the right to die are quick to propose that a government sponsored and controlled national health care program would be the best means of allocating health care resources. Since individuals can't be expected or trusted to make fair allocation decisions with respect to their own medical care, it should be left to the government to make such decisions. However, where do the government decision makers come from—another planet? Will depraved bureaucrats somehow make better decisions than depraved private citizens?

We cannot expect justice from a program of national health insurance that produces serious inequities and injustices in the Medicaid and Medicare programs. Care givers and patients are unsatisfied with both programs. How would expanding it to 250 million people improve it? How would regulating health care by government fiat eliminate the waste and gaming of the system?

TREATING HEALTH AS A MORAL ISSUE

One possible solution for Christians is to apply the principles governing stewardship to medical care. That entails making health a moral issue for Christians, which the church has not done as yet. Yet our theology teaches that man is a unified being, body and spirit. We acknowledge that we function as an integrated being and that our emotions have an impact on our physical well-being.

Would a church ignore anyone suffering from an obvious personality disorder, particularly if the individual's mental state manifested itself through outbursts during church services? Would leaders ignore a church member who was physically acting out her anger with threats or acts of violence? If a Christian is irresponsible with his finances to the point of coming to the church for help, would church leaders offer financial assistance with no questions asked? It would be within the parameters of good spiritual leadership to help such a person get his finances under control. Should we do any less when an individual is chronically ill or manifests ongoing medical problems?

That is not to suggest that every illness should be linked to a particular sin or that church leaders should attempt to extract a confession from every sick person they visit. However, when a Christian is using a sizable amount of medical resources for chronic medical conditions it is not outside our spiritual responsibilities to find out why.

In recent years the government has undertaken efforts to improve the nation's health. Anti-smoking campaigns have reduced the number of people dying from diseases associated with smoking. The emphasis upon physical exercise and diet is beginning to pay dividends. People are beginning to realize that public awareness can reduce drug use, contributing to better health for many. In the near future, society may also rediscover the long-term health benefits of faithful, monogamous sex as the church has preached for years.

Although the church has made behavior-based health an issue for years, the emphasis has been on character more than on health. Smoking was framed more as a character issue than a health concern. Although a person's health was one of the reasons marshaled against smoking, it was not the premiere reason. For many, smoking is antithetical to Christian character. The fact that it is unhealthy only strengthens the case against it. However, the "character issue" concerning smoking is almost entirely cultural. Many Christians still raise and market tobacco, and their churches accept tithes and offerings from the profits.

Preaching against drinking alcoholic beverages because of the personal, social, and familial devastation they often cause should be followed up with programs to help those struggling with an alcohol problem.

The church should present its opposition to drinking, smoking, illicit sex, substance abuse, and so on, as based on threats to total health—physical, emotional, and spiritual—thereby demonstrating serious concern for the whole person. The success of crisis pregnancy centers (CPC) in addressing the issue of unwelcome pregnancy indicates that the potential is enormous. Hundreds of women each year come to faith in Christ through the ministry of crisis pregnancy centers as they receive practical assistance in caring for their children. The CPC serves as a model for other ministries aimed at medical problems that are behavior based. Who can predict what evangelistic possibilities may come from similar efforts?

Christians have given medical technology a far greater role in their lives and lifestyles than they ought. Sin has consequences, but modern medicine has developed numerous ways to "fix" or suppress the consequences so that people do not feel compelled to change behavior. "Values neutral" medicine is as much a part of the problem as the behavior itself. Rather than teaching young women not to engage in illicit sex, physicians prescribe birth control devices. In doing so they convey that the worst consequence of sexual involvement outside of marriage is pregnancy. Such medical advice betrays both women and society because it proposes a medical solution to a moral problem. Similarly, Christians often utilize medicine to minimize the consequences of sinful behavior rather than changing their behavior.

Likewise, placing an individual who has spent a lifetime systematically destroying his body by smoking, using alcohol, and so on high on an organ transplant waiting list sends the message that physical problems are unrelated to character and behavior. Providing cosmetic breast implants to a woman who desires to improve her career as an exotic dancer also stretches the concept of medical need and communicates the fallacy that the human body can be appropriately seen as a source of entertainment.

TOWARD A CHRISTIAN APPROACH TO HEALTH CARE ALLOCATION

Christians should set the pace for the rest of society by exercising good stewardship of health care resources. Behaviors that lead to health problems should be avoided—smoking, overeating, lack of sleep, substance abuse, illicit sex. Perhaps people who commit themselves to avoiding high-risk behaviors should form their own health maintenance organizations, both as a way to control medical costs and as a model for society.

Since our lives on earth are temporary, there seems to be little support in Christian theology for the notion that every individual has a moral claim to unlimited health care resources. Ultimately, our trust must not rest in human resources but in God. Therefore, as the apostle Paul stated, "For if we live, we live for the Lord, or if we die, we die for the Lord; therefore whether we live or die, we are the Lord's" (Romans 14:8).

We can look to the example of the Lord Jesus Christ in His earthly ministry. He possessed the power to heal every disease in Israel but didn't. In fact, as His earthly ministry progressed, He engaged less in healing and more in teaching. If the goal of perfect health were valid biblically, it appears that many fell short of it at a time when the Great Physician was in their midst.

Terminally ill patients do not have an unlimited right to health care resources. It is a misapplication of stewardship principles for a Christian to demand them to extend his or her earthly life briefly when unable to pay for that care, and when others could benefit from the resources more. Does that weaken our commitment to the sanctity of human life? Not necessarily; it merely acknowledges the limitations of medicine.

Of course we should not fail to treat the terminally ill person with respect and dignity. It would be morally repugnant to treat her like a worn-out piece of machinery lacking social value and, therefore, not worthy to receive the investment of medical care. However, care givers and family need to recognize that continued medical treatment may offer only marginal benefit.

We may also need to emphasize preventive care, such as immunizations, periodic testing, and other routine physical examinations. That would fall within the realm of public health and could potentially be managed by government agencies or private providers.

It is difficult to maintain that each individual has a moral right to unlimited access to all health care resources, especially when resources are scarce or when others have a stronger moral claim to them. For example, does a patient in the end stages of cancer have an equal moral claim to expensive chemotherapy, where there is only a 20 percent chance of surviving another three months, as a person who has just been diagnosed with the same type of cancer and could potentially live much longer ? Suppose the first individual is the governor of a state and the latter a truck mechanic. Should a person's position in society affect medical resource allocation?

CONCLUSION

As a society we are only in the early stages of the debate over the allocation of health care resources. Many questions will not have easy answers. Within the Christian community fundamental questions remain to be discussed.

Once again I would call upon the Christian community to demonstrate leadership in this debate. We cannot afford to merely respond to the proposals of secularists or to be content to discuss the issues on their terms. We must make our best case and be willing to follow through on the implications.

QUESTIONS TO THINK ABOUT

1. Who owns medical resources, and are those resources morally special, or do they fall under the category of consumer products available for purchase?
2. Under what circumstances, if any, should age or "quality of life" be considered in allocating health care resources?
3. Should a Christian receive medical care for elective medical procedures when he does not have the personal resources to pay for it?
4. Is it morally acceptable for a physician to provide a terminally ill patient with only the medical care he can afford?
5. Are physicians required to be uncompromising advocates for their patients, or can they be expected to serve the interests of a third party, for example, a health insurance company or hospital?

NOTES

Chapter 3: Conception Control and Family Size

1. Cited in John J. Davis, *Evangelical Ethics* (Philipsburg, N.J.: Presb. & Ref., 1985), p. 44.
2. W. Cates, letter to John Mackey, Ad Hoc Committee in Defense of life, January 4, 1977.
3. Ronald L. Kleinman, ed., *Hormonal Contraception* (London: Int. Planned Parenthood, 1990), p. 60.
4. William Webster et al. v. Reproductive Health Services et al., 88 U.S. 605 (1989).
5. Kleinman, p. 97.
6. Ibid., p. 100. Also see S. J. Segal et al., "Norplant implants: the mechanism of contraceptive action," *Fertility and Sterility* 56, no. 2 (August 1991), pp. 273-77.
7. See George Grant, *Grand Illusions: The Legacy of Planned Parenthood* (Brentwood, Tenn.: Wolgemuth & Hyatt, 1988), pp. 41ff.

Chapter 4: Fetal Experimentation

1. *National Right to Life News* (December 1988): 7.
2. Turtox-Cambosco catalog, 1976, cited in Suzanne M. Rini, *Beyond Abortion: A Chronicle of Fetal Experimentation* (Avon-by-the-Sea, N.J.: Magnificat, 1988), p. 36.
3. For an in-depth look at fetal experimentation, see Rini, *Beyond Abortion*, p. 186.
4. Saul Bellow, *U.S. News and World Report*, June 28, 1982, p. 49, cited in *National Right to Life News*, November 24, 1982.

Chapter 5: Infertility and Medically Assisted Procreation

1. _Infertility: Medical and Social Choices_, Congress of the United States, Office of Science and Technology, U.S. Government Printing Office, Washington, D.C. (May 1988), p. 5.

2. Willard Cates, Division of Sexually Transmitted Diseases, National Centers for Disease Control, Atlanta, GA. (April 28, 1987). Cited in _Infertility: Medical and Social Choices_, p. 61.

3. _Infertility: Medical and Social Choices_, p. 126.

4. Leon Kass, "New Beginnings in Life," cited in Michael Hamilton, ed., _The New Genetics and the Future of Man_ (Grand Rapids: Eerdmans, 1972), p. 55.

5. Cited in Richard Neuhaus, "The Return of Eugenics," _Commentary_ (April 1988), p. 16.

6. "Top Celebs of the Decade," _People_, March 5, 1984, p. 73.

7. Fern S. Chapman, "Going for the Gold in the Baby Business," _Fortune_, September 17, 1984, p. 41.

8. Committee on Ethics, "Multifetal Pregnancy Reduction and Selective Fetal Termination," American College of Obstetricians and Gynecologists Committee Opinion, no. 94 (April 1991), pp. 1-3.

Chapter 6: Severely Handicapped Newborns

1. Jeff Lyon, _Playing God in the Nursery_ (New York: Norton, 1985), p. 33.

2. J. Arras et al., "The Effect of New Pediatric Capabilities and the Problem of Uncertainty," _Hastings Center Report_ 17, no. 6 (December 1987): 10.

3. R. R. Faden et al., "Prenatal Screening and Pregnant Women's Attitudes Toward the Abortion of Defective Fetuses," _American Journal of Public Health_ 77, no. 3 (March 1987): 290.

4. D. Tordes et al., "Pediatricians' Attitudes Affecting Decision Making in Defective Newborns," _Pediatrics_ 60 (October 1977): 197-201.

5. A. Shaw et al., "Ethical Issues in Pediatric Surgery: A National Survey of Pediatricians and Pediatric Surgeons," _Pediatrics_ 60 (October 1977): 588-99.

6. R. Duff and A. G. M. Campbell, "On Deciding the Care of Severely Handicapped or Dying Persons: With Particular Reference to Infants," _Pediatrics_ 57 (April 1976): 492.

7. M. Tooley, "A Defense of Abortion and Infanticide," in _The Problem of Abortion_, Joel Feinberg, ed. (Belmont, Calif.: Wadsworth, 1973), p. 60.

Chapter 8: Genetic Engineering

1. See Mark I. Evans and Mark Paul Johnson, "Chorion Villus Sampling" in *Reproductive Risks and Prenatal Diagnosis*, Mark I. Evans, ed. (Norwalk, Conn.: Appleton & Lange, 1992), p. 178.
2. See Evans, *Reproductive Risks*, p. 179.
3. Forum: "Ethics in Embryo," *Harper's*, September 1987, p. 42.

Chapter 12: The Allocation and Rationing of Health Care

1. Leonard Fleck, "Just Health Care: The Nexus of Public Policy and Institutional Policy," Medical Ethics for the 1990s Conference, Michigan State University (August 11-16, 1991).
2. Daniel Callahan, "Terminating Treatment: Age as a Standard," *Hastings Center Report* (October-November 1987): 25.

BIBLIOGRAPHY

Anderson, Bruce L. *The Price of a Perfect Baby.* Minneapolis: Bethany, 1984.

Anonymous. *Daddy, I'm Pregnant.* Portland: Multnomah, 1987.

Beisner, E. Calvin. *Prospects for Growth: A Biblical View of Population, Resources, and the Future.* Westchester, Ill.: Crossway, 1990.

Burtchaell, James T. *Rachel Weeping: The Case Against Abortion.* San Francisco: Harper & Row, 1982.

Chilton, David. *Productive Christians in an Age of Guilt Manipulators.* Tyler, Tex.: Institute for Christian Economics, 1981.

Davis, John Jefferson. *Evangelical Ethics: Issues Facing the Church Today.* Phillipsburg, N.J.: Presb. & Ref., 1985.

Evans, Debra. *Without Moral Limits: Women, Reproduction and the New Medical Technology.* Westchester, Ill.: Crossway, 1989.

Evans, Mark I., ed. *Reproductive Risks and Prenatal Diagnosis.* Norwalk, Conn.: Appleton & Lange, 1992.

Glessner, Thomas A. *Achieving an Abortion-Free America by 2001.* Portland: Multnomah, 1990.

Grant, George. *Grand Illusions: The Legacy of Planned Parenthood.* Brentwood, Tenn.: Wolgemuth & Hyatt, 1988.

————. *Third Time Around: A History of the Pro-Life Movement from the First Century to the Present.* Brentwood, Tenn.: Wolgemuth & Hyatt, 1991.

Horan, Dennis J., and Melinda Delahoyde, eds. *Infanticide and the Handicapped Newborn.* Provo, Utah: Brigham Young, 1982.

Kasun, Jacqueline. *The War Against Population: The Economics and Ideology of Population Control.* San Francisco: St. Ignatius, 1988.

Koop, C. Everett. *The Right to Live, The Right to Die.* Wheaton, Ill.: Tyndale, 1976.

Koop, C. Everett, and Francis A. Schaeffer. *Whatever Happened to the Human Race?* Westchester, Ill.: Crossway, 1980.

Lifton, Robert Jay. *The Nazi Doctors: Medical Killing and the Psychology of Genocide.* New York: Basic Books, 1986.

Lyon, Jeff. *Playing God in the Nursery.* New York: Norton, 1985.

McIlhaney, Joseph. *Safe Sex: A Doctor Explains the Risks and Reality of AIDS and Other Sexually Transmitted Diseases.* Grand Rapids: Baker, 1990.

Nelson, Leonard J., ed. *The Death Decision.* Ann Arbor, Mich.: Servant, 1984.

Neuhaus, Richard John, ed. *Guaranteeing the Good Life: Medicine and the Return of Eugenics.* Grand Rapids: Eerdmans, 1990.

Noonan, John T. *A Private Choice: Abortion in America in the Seventies.* Toronto: Life Cycle, 1979.

Olasky, Marvin. *The Press and Abortion, 1838-1988.* Hillsdale, N.J.: Lawrence Erlbaum, 1988.

Payne, Franklin E. *Biblical Medical Ethics: The Christian and the Practice of Medicine.* Milford, Mich.: Mott Media, 1985.

————. *Making Biblical Decisions.* Escondido, Calif.: Hosanna House, 1989.

Rini, Suzanne M. *Beyond Abortion: A Chronicle of Fetal Experimentation.* Avon-by-the-Sea, N.J.: Magnificat, 1988.

Rorvik, David. *In His Image: The Cloning of a Man.* New York: Lippincott, 1978.

Selby, Terry L. *The Mourning After: Help for the Postabortion Syndrome.* Grand Rapids: Baker, 1990.

Shettles, Landrum, and David Rorvik. *Rites of Life: The Scientific Evidence for Life Before Birth.* Grand Rapids: Zondervan, 1983.

Smith, F. LaGard. *When Choice Becomes God.* Eugene, Oreg.: Harvest House, 1990.

Weir, Robert. *Selective Nontreatment of Handicapped Newborns.* New York: Oxford Univ., 1984.

Wennberg, Robert N. *Terminal Choices: Euthanasia, Suicide, and the Right to Die.* Grand Rapids: Eerdmans, 1989.

Young, Curt. *The Least of These: What Everyone Should Know About Abortion.* Chicago: Moody, 1983.

Moody Press, a ministry of the Moody Bible Institute,
is designed for education, evangelization, and edification.
If we may assist you in knowing more about Christ
and the Christian life, please write us without obligation:
Moody Press, c/o MLM, Chicago, Illinois 60610.